Acclaim for Paul Cummins' Previous Books

Dachau Song: The Twentieth Century Odyssey of Herbert Zipper
"I read the book with growing suspense. It is written with crystal clarity and with knowledge of European dimensions rarely found among Americans."
—Sebastian Feldman,
Rheinische Post, Dusseldorf, Germany

For Mortal Stakes: Solutions for Schools and Society
"My father, Ralph Abernathy, and my 'Uncle Martin' Luther King would have applauded Paul Cummins, his books, his life's work, and his profound contributions to humanity, as I have."
—Donzaleigh Abernathy,
Actress and Human Rights Activist

"*For Mortal Stakes* is rich with ideas and solutions to many of our most troublesome school problems. Educators and citizens alike will find it inspiring."
—Ted Danson,
Actor and Environmental Activist

"Cummins offers new visions of education and proven paths to realize those visions."
—Jonathan Kozol

Keeping Watch: Reflections on American Culture, Education and Politics
"A visionary in education who has brought about a bridge for different ethnic minorities to get quality education . . ."
—Arianna Huffington

". . . daring innovation and commitment to the creative process . . ."
—Robert Scheer

A Postcard from Bali (Poetry)
"What one finds when reading Paul Cummins' poetry is that there is no difference between what he does with his poetry and the rest of his life."
—Ann Colburn

Proceed with Passion: Engaging Students in Meaningful Education
"As a parent of children studying in a school founded by Paul Cummins, I have observed at first hand the reasons why he is a unique asset to American education. Into this book, he has distilled both the passion and the careful reasoning behind his successes.
—Jared Dia

Two Americas
Two Educations

Funding Quality Schools for All Students

Paul F. Cummins

RED HEN PRESS | Los Angeles, California

Two Americas, Two Educations:
Funding Quality Schools for All Children

Book design by Mark E. Cull
Cover design by Wendy Bryan
Production assistance: Richard O. Niño

ISBN-10: 1-59709-688-1
ISBN-13: 978-1-59709-688-1
Library of Congress Catalog Card Number: 2006928350

The City of Los Angeles Department of Cultural Affairs,
Los Angeles County Arts Commission
and the National Endowment for the Arts
partially support Red Hen Press.

Published by Red Hen Press

First Edition

To underserved, neglected children everywhere whose suffering is unnecessary.

In memory of my sister, Camille (Mimi) Ruth Cummins Adams, (October 28, 1933-March 5, 2006), whose loyalty and love of her family was matched by her care for humanity.

Acknowledgements

Because this book is largely about finance and funding, I want, initially, to thank several people who over the years have helped me wander through this arcane and labyrinthine world. I will simply list them alphabetically since what each has contributed to my education would be a chapter in itself:

Jackie Bly
Chuck Boxenbaum
Jean Campbell
Richard Crowell
Joel Landau
Alva Libuser
Herbert (Bill) Lucas
Adrienne McCandless
David W. Newman
Robert Scheer
John Shank
Nat Trives

Also, I want to thank several people for reading earlier drafts and for making helpful suggestions – Ken Adams, Mike Babcock, Mickey Bearman, Douglas Browne, Anna and Emily Cummins, Paul Kanin, Brian Milinsky and Nathan Reynolds. A close reading of several drafts for the second time in two years was provided by Nadia Lawrence, whose proofing skills are superb. And to N.B. for her multiple mitzvahs.

Given my own techno challenges – or as my daughters characterize it, my Neanderthal leanings – my assistant Jackie Stehr typed numerous drafts of each chapter, made intelligent suggestions and stylistic improvements, and helped in countless other ways.

Also, I want to thank several people who have broadened my understanding of social inequities and of the true meaning of inclusion. This list is long, but certainly it includes: Fred Ali, Carol Biondi, Andy Bogen, Moctesuma Esparza, Rafe Esquith, Shari Foos, Jo Kaplan, Phillip Lance, Leslie Gilbert-Lurie, Anita Landecker, George Molsbarger, Nancy London, Joe Perez, Fernando Rodriguez, Deanne Shartin, Bill Siart, Lee Walcott, Tony Walker, and Jack Zimmerman. I hasten to add, the ideas in this book are my own and any limitations are not attributable to the people I have acknowledged.

Finally, I want to thank Kate Gale and Mark Cull, the wonderful co-creators of Red Hen Press, for their faith in me, their editorial support, and their commitment to writers and to making this a better society.

Contents

IV CREATING NEW SOURCES OF REVENUE

Preface

Nearly everyone in America, no matter what political persuasion, would agree that as a nation we need to have adequate public schools. In fact, nearly everyone would also agree that our schools should be more than merely adequate: they should be superior.

Needless to say, at the moment U.S. public schools are not superior—and sadly, many of them are not even adequate. As a nation, can we make the commitment to improving our schools to the point at which they can truthfully be called superior? Can we agree to assign a high priority to the tasks necessary to improve the schools, then demand that funds be allocated to accomplish them? The general public may be unsure of the answers to these questions, but I believe the proper answer is a resounding, "Yes!"

First we would have to agree on definitions of "quality," "excellence," and "adequacy." For example, by "adequate" do we mean quite sufficient, or do we mean acceptable—but with connotations of mediocre? Either way, adequate does not suggest superior. If we truly want superior schools, we will have to identify the resources that will be necessary to fund them properly.

This book will grapple with all these questions. First, I will describe what superb, or even simply adequate, schools would look like, and second, how those schools might be funded. The book is designed for general readers, educators, and lawmakers. It is not intended to be a final blueprint, but only a series of suggestive possibilities. I leave it for legislative, tax, and finance experts to supply the details of how to implement these ideas should they ever be accepted as reasonable or even compelling. For now, I present the case for superb schools and explain how they can become a reality.

I would offer, further, the notion that there is a positive and an active hunger within the soul for justice. I believe that once we are offered a vision of justice that includes the individual as the active and effective agent of his or her participation in that vision, there is no going back: we will henceforth, however inarticulately, suffer from that hunger.

—c.k. williams

Part I

What Is, What Could Be, What Should Be

If our America now is a petty shambles
Of disillusion and violence
The dreams of its possibility stay actual ...
                              —Robert Creeley

CHAPTER 1

The Way We Were,
The Way We Are

There must be a passion to end
poverty, for nothing less than that will do.
—Michael Harrington

There is one issue all Americans agree upon. We all say we believe in the value of education. Whatever our political or economic views, whatever our varied cultural orientations and tastes, whatever our religious convictions, we all believe that high-quality education is critical to the individual and to society. This means that we share a fundamental belief that public education has the capacity to mold the nation's young people into capable, productive, and decent citizens, and that this accomplishment is one of our country's highest public goals, if not *the* supreme goal.

Yet many of our schools are failing. How has this tragic disconnect occurred? Daily in our newspapers we read of declining test scores, overcrowded schools, gangs and vandalism, drugs and violence, deteriorating school grounds and buildings, alienated youth who are dropping out in droves. Yet, during much of this time, say, 1970–2005, the U.S. economy has grown and flourished. California, whose economy is larger than that of most nations in the world, is a case in point. In the 1970s, California public schools were judged to be excellent. Per-pupil spending in California schools was consistently above the national average. Then several major challenges (some would say disasters) confronted the state, and thus the schools, simultaneously.

California began receiving an unprecedented influx of immigrants, who now constitute 10 percent of the population (as opposed to the national average of 5 percent). Many of the new immigrants, who spoke little English, enrolled their children in the public schools. (Latino children now represent 45.8 percent of California's public schools and 72.8 percent of the Los Angeles Unified School District.) In addition, California has one of the highest percentages in the nation of children who live in poverty, and this condition is worsening.

A second blow was the passage in 1978 of Proposition 13, a statewide referendum that deliberately lowered the state's property tax revenue. Gradually California's previously admirable per-pupil funding fell to third lowest in the nation—where it has remained. English language learners and children living in poverty are simply more expensive to educate. California is not the only state to fail to respond to this demand upon its resources. California is a blatant example, but the rest of the nation is also failing. Not everything is a matter of funding, but funding is a crucial issue. While some conservatives, such as Eric Hanusher, point out that correlating funding to achievement is murky, [1] the noted educator Alfie Kohn points out that no one in the suburbs says, "Money isn't correlated with achievement, so here, you may as well take some of this extra cash off our hands." [2] Even the most cautious of studies indicates that funding levels are crucial to student performance. In a recent study, Anne L. Jefferson concludes: "Overall, the literature indicates that the amount of money cannot be removed as an important variable in the education achievement of students. Furthermore, the literature clearly points to usage of money allocated as key." [3] Our nation's inner-city and low-income neighborhoods and impoverished rural communities are being grossly ignored, under funded, and thereby harmed. Writing about an often ignored segment of our nation—that is, poor rural areas—Cynthia Duncan states that nearly nine million Americans live in poverty in rural areas and one-third of the nine million live in communities with persistently high poverty rates. These children are virtually invisible; without a high-quality education, their chances to escape the crippling effects of poverty are almost nil. As Duncan writes, "Education is, just as the American Dream has always implied, an avenue for upward mobility for individuals. But most schools in America's poor communities do not offer that opportunity." [4]

The nation also faces a growing sense that democracy at home is under siege. No matter how much they may admire billionaire captains of industry, most Americans still cherish a belief in a just society that is able to maintain at least some equality or proportionality of opportunity, and appropriateness in the distribution of wealth. Yet, as we have seen—and as this book argues—there has been a relatively recent and very rapid increase in the disparity of wealth in America. This growing gap plays itself out in our national education systems, where we see the growth of two distinct polarities: two Americas, two educations. On the one hand we see private schools and wealthy neighborhood public schools that offer beautiful and functional campuses, comprehensive and enriched curricula, and excellent teaching conditions. On the other hand, we find many inner-city and low-income neighborhood public schools with inadequate facilities, overcrowded classrooms, undernourished curricula, and overall miserable teaching conditions. And though some would argue otherwise, the fact that the well-to-do schools are often spending three times more than the others is, I believe, a major reason for the differences in quality, and hence opportunity, for the children. There is an elephant in the living room that most legislators, citizens, and even educators are ignoring: we are not properly funding our schools. Though we may wish it would, this elephant will not go away. Furthermore, there is a reason for this situation that we have not yet fully grasped.

Some will argue that educational spending has grown along with everything else—so what's the problem? They will often add that it must therefore be poor management, bureaucracy, progressively oriented college education departments, or whatever, that have rendered our schools inadequate, not a lack of funds. I disagree. What we have not grasped is that in urban areas and elsewhere there has been a massive increase in social problems that has been neither fully acknowledged nor confronted.

This proliferation of social problems receives lip service, but few realize the impact of these problems upon schools. Consider: a massive infusion of non-English-speaking students—in some schools more than 50 languages are spoken. Consider: in some neighborhoods there are two and three families living in one- or two-bedroom apartments whose conditions afford students no possibility of studying or doing homework. Consider: in many of these neighborhoods gangs rule, and from 3 p.m. to darkness the streets and parks are unsafe. Where then do inner-city children go and what can they do? Consider: in many neighborhoods drug dealing, crime, and violence are daily occurrences; consequently many children come to school frightened, sometimes abused, or physically undernourished. The pitifully understaffed schools are expected to deal with these problems as well as teaching academic skills—and, frequently, all of this is expected to be carried out in overcrowded classrooms.

The implications and requirements that these relatively new social conditions impose on schools are enormous. To make serious improvements would necessitate:

1. in many middle schools and high schools, cutting class size in half, which would necessitate
2. hiring 100 percent more teachers—which would necessitate
3. repairing campuses and building more schools and classrooms and
4. hiring more counselors, special education specialists, ESL teachers and
5. creating after-school programs for latchkey children and youth.

That would be just a start. Yet each of these requirements would require substantial new funding. There's that elephant.

But for some reason the elephant seems to be invisible. Poverty and its companions, poor health systems, poor housing, and poor schools, seem to be off society's radar screen. Forty-five years ago Michael Harrington noted that "The other America, the America of poverty, is hidden today in a way that it never was before. Its millions are socially invisible to the rest of us." [5] Similarly, a year before Harrington, James Bryant Conant argued in his *Slums and Suburbs* that "The contrast in money available to schools in a wealthy suburb and to the schools in a large city jolts one's notions of the meaning of equality of opportunity." [6]

As concerned as Conant and Harrington may have been in 1961–62, matters have worsened since then. Furthermore, studies have demonstrated that inner-city children, rather than the smaller per-pupil funding they receive, actually require more funds in order to compensate for their social deprivation. Bruce D. Baker, a reviewer of several such studies, concludes that children from economically deprived backgrounds would require 35 percent more spending than the average costs, and children with limited English proficiency will require spending around 100 percent above average.[7] Anything short of this amount is likely to perpetuate failure.

A recent Rand Corporation study that was commissioned to discover the complex reasons behind California's underperformance in K–12 education reached several important conclusions.[8] First, California's per-pupil expenditures were third lowest in the nation, as mentioned earlier in this chapter. Reasoning that perhaps one explanation for California's difficulties could be found in its disproportionate number of immigrants, the Rand economists statistically corrected for this disparity among the states. This time, California's expenditures came out dead last! But then a completely unexpected result emerged: Texas, with a similarly large minority population, which had languished along with California near the bottom of the per-pupil spending rankings, vaulted to first place when the data was adjusted for minority enrollments. In other words, unlike California, Texas has actually faced up to the challenge of trying to provide a decent education to non-English-speaking children and children of poverty, primarily by means of universal preschool for low-income children. As Rand's lead economist explained in a recent briefing, this achievement was driven almost entirely by Texas' business leaders who, to their credit, realized that providing a substandard education to Texas' low-income and non-English-speaking students would in the long run immensely impair Texas' economic prospects and its competitiveness. It does not even require an extra helping of the milk of human kindness to see that funding public education adequately is the correct thing; in the case of the Texas business community, even simple self-interest will do.

The consequences attached to failing or succeeding in this gigantic effort are enormous. In a real sense, both our nation's soul and its essential viability are at stake. If we become a hopelessly and irreversibly two-tiered society with the few very rich flourishing and the many poor living in degraded conditions, we will have shattered the American dream of a democratic, just, and fair society. We will have become an oligarchy–aristocracy–plutocracy, but will no longer be a democracy. How we regard and treat our schools will be a major determinant of what path we choose. We are already well down the road towards oligarchy; it is almost too late to change. Almost.

NOTES:

1 Eric Hanusher, as quoted in Alfie Kohn, *The Schools Our Children Deserve.* (New York: Houghton Mifflin Company, 1999), p. 247.

2 Ibid.

3 Anne L. Jefferson, "Student Performance: Is More Money the Answer?" *Journal of Education Finance,* Fall 2002, pp. 111–124.

4 Cynthia Duncan, 2000. *Worlds Apart: Why Poverty Persists in Rural America.* (Cambridge, MA: Yale University Press), p. 205.

5 Michael Harrington, *The Other America.* (New York, Penguin Books, 1962), p. 3.

6 James Bryant Conant, 1961 *Slums and Suburbs.* New York: Signet, p. 10.

7 Bruce D. Baker, "The Emerging Shape of Educational Adequacy." *Journal of Education Finance.* Winter 2005, pp. 259–287.

8 Stephen J. Carroll et al., *California's K–12 Public Schools: How Are They Doing?* The Rand Corporation, RAND/MG-186-EDU, 2005.

CHAPTER 2

Adequacy: What Is It?

*Without imagining justice
there could be no justice.*
—Medgar Evers

In the never-ending debate about how well the nation's public schools perform, several intertwined issues are always present:

Adequacy—whether the schools have been given enough resources to do their job.

Equity—whether the schools' funding sources (local, state, or federal revenues, or exceptional revenues such as the proceeds from lotteries) are distributed fairly between poor and rich districts.

Accountability—whether the schools deliver a reasonable educational outcome given the funds allocated to them.

Recently, as states have wrestled with funding and allocating funding sources, the issue of adequacy has largely been pursued in state courts, in individual or class-action lawsuits instigated to argue that certain funding arrangements are so low that specific school districts are impaired in their ability to deliver a respectable educational outcome.

What Is An "Adequate" School?
As imprecise as the term may be, we can establish a few obvious criteria. (By the way, these criteria must apply to *all* schools, whether in high-poverty districts or affluent suburbs.)

Decent Facilities
♦ Toilets that flush

- Clean halls and classrooms
- A desk for each child or student
- Well-functioning lighting, heat and air-conditioning
- Playgrounds with level fields and functioning equipment
- Daily maintenance and security, as well as weekend security

Sufficient Materials
- Up-to-date textbooks (one for each child)
- Paperback literature for each student to take home as assigned reading
- Labs with enough supplies and equipment
- Preferably a school library with up-to-date holdings

Reasonable Class Size and Teacher Load
- 4 to 5 classes a day of 20 students in each class (5 to 6 classes a day of 30–50 students in each class is defined as not reasonable)

Secondary School Teachers Teaching Subjects in Which They Have a Degree
- For example, history should be taught by history majors, not P.E. teachers filling out their daily hours
- Specialists should be available for non-core curricula

Diverse and Comprehensive Curricula
- Math, science, history, English, and languages
- In addition, courses in the arts, physical education, academic and arts electives, after-school teams and clubs, arts performances, and the like

Adequacy cases go back more than 30 years now in over 30 states in America. One early case, *Robinson v. Cahill,* was tried in New Jersey in 1973. In this case the court held that property taxes were an unfair basis of funding education, since they discriminated against children in poor districts. The court ruled that the state had to design a fairer means of funding.

As other states would soon discover, the New Jersey court orders set in motion a political storm that continues to this day. Raising taxes, redistributing taxpayers' money from rich to poor districts, court-mandated curriculum reforms and programs, massive school construction programs, expansion of schooling to full-day kindergartens and preschools: these and many other requirements imposed by the courts led to judicial and legislative battles. In many cases, states were forced to look closely at statewide shortcomings in education and, in particular, to shine light on the deficiencies in the education of poor children.

Adequacy cases often center on equity. In Ohio, as in so many other states, the issue was the gap in per-pupil spending between wealthy and poor districts. Of course, the folly of funding education through property tax revenues was at the eye of the storm. As Peter Schrag pointed out, "In 1993, the Cleveland suburb of Cuyahoga Heights, with a $22 million (2.2 percent) property tax levy, could spend $12,000 per pupil; East Cleveland, *taxing itself at triple that rate,* could spend just over $5,500." [1] For this and other related reasons, a series of court cases were filed (1997, 2000, 2001, 2002). In the first *Derolph v. State [of Ohio],* 1997, the court delivered the following message:

> Ohio's public financing scheme must undergo a complete systematic overhaul . . . which must eliminate the emphasis of Ohio's school funding system on local property tax.

The court added:

> A thorough and efficient system of common schools includes facilities in good repair and the supplies, materials, and funds necessary to maintain these facilities in a safe manner, in compliance with all local, state and federal mandates. [2]

Of course, courts can issue pronouncements of what should be, but legislatures need to create the means of implementation. Political squabbling and legislative reaction led to a second Derolph case 2001 reiterating the need for systematic overhaul, which in turn was virtually ignored by a Republican-dominated legislature. Consequently, inequities in statewide funding and disparities of educational quality persist in Ohio.

To be sure, Ohio is not unique. In many other cases state courts have issued directives, and even maps, for legislatures to follow. These directives have not only ordered systemic changes in funding methods, but have also spelled out specific educational and curricular mandates. Some legislatures have tried to comply; others have stalled, delayed, or outright refused. Sometimes a new round of court cases will ensue while children continue to receive *in*adequate education.

A recent case in Austin, Texas is a clear example of the yo-yo process: the courts rule in favor of plaintiffs seeking educational redress; the legislatures cry poor; and the defendants—often the states—appeal the process. For example, on September 15, 2004, a Texas district judge, John Dietz, "declared the state's beleaguered funding system unconstitutional largely because it fails to close the achievement gap between white and minority students." [3] The judge declared that Texas failed to raise enough money to provide "an adequate suitable education" as the state constitution provides. And, of course, the decision was immediately appealed. Notable also was the failure of the legislature in 2003 to pass a school finance overhaul.

A recent case in California was *Williams v. State of California*, litigated by the American Civil Liberties Union. This case was brought to trial in order to argue that the California legislature, in its nearly Dickensian definition of "adequacy" (e.g., that a school failing to provide one textbook per pupil could still be considered "adequate"), was incompetent to be assigned the determination of adequacy.

Not only do great disparities in funding exist across the country, but a study released in 2004 by the Education Trust (a research group that supports the federal "Leave No Child Behind" law) revealed that "The financial gap between poor and wealthy districts has widened . . ." [4] High-poverty districts (the 2002 database—the most recent available) typically received $868 per pupil less than districts with fewer poor children. And in one of the nation's most populous states, Illinois, for example, the gap was $2,026 per pupil. These disparities account in large part for the inadequacy of many programs.

Professor Bruce D. Baker provides a rich, comprehensive overview of studies dealing with the relationship of spending costs to achieving adequate education in our schools. Among his findings, not so surprising are that the following assumptions are true:

1. Additional resources are positively associated with student outcomes.

2. Costs associated with achieving high average student outcomes are higher than the costs associated with achieving low average student outcomes.
3. The cost of achieving high outcome standards can be quite high.
4. Children classified as having higher costs associated with their educational needs most often include children from economically deprived backgrounds and children with English language communication barriers (these costs range from 35 percent to 100 percent more).
5. The overall quality of the teacher pool is contingent on the overall level of available wages.
6. Higher poverty concentrations in very large districts tend to lead to greater increases in the cost of outcomes.
7. Poor urban schools with high concentrations of poverty have the most difficulty recruiting and retaining high-quality teachers and may have to pay substantially higher wages to attract and retain them. [5]

What I find bizarre and depressing is that in almost all of the court cases and scholarly examinations of how to fund adequate education, the definition of "adequacy" is so minimal. Consequently, arguments about increasing revenues even by small amounts do not set revenue standards to where they would have to be to go beyond the bare minimum. *Superior* schools should be the goal, not just a vision of "adequacy," with watered-down, anemic curricula, underpaid teachers, inadequate facilities, and the like. The highest public school per-pupil expenditures in the country are still about 50 percent *less* than in high-quality private schools.

The five criteria mentioned at the beginning of the chapter seem so self-evident as to not require mentioning. Each, however, is sadly missing in many schools across the country, which are located mostly in inner-city and poor immigrant neighborhoods. Their absence is a major impetus driving the various lawsuits that have occurred in state after state—California, New Jersey, Ohio, Kentucky, Alabama, North Carolina, Maryland, and New York, for example.

In a recent article in *Education Week* written by an attorney who has represented the defendant states in many cases, Alfred A. Lindseth argues against the value of these cases. He writes that these cases deflect attention from education reform to such issues as: "Where is the money going to come from? Is it going to be taken from other school districts? If so, which ones? What non-education programs will have to be cut? What portion of the increased costs will be borne by local taxpayers?" [6] Apparently it never occurs to Mr. Lindseth, a senior partner in a law firm, that the funds might come from somewhere other than local taxpayers or from cuts in services.

Many critics of the educational scene argue that the real issue is not money, "but . . ." The "but" clause will differ each time. Some will say it is poor management. We have enough money, the argument runs, we are simply not managing it properly. Others argue that we need to provide vouchers for parents to use in choosing the school to which they want to send their child. [7] Others argue for greater privatization of our schools along the line of, say, the Edison schools. [8]

This book takes a different and generally unpopular position. We are not spending enough per pupil, and our public schools' failures *are* a result of inadequate spending. It is worth noting that charter schools, which often revolve around a particular theme or philosophy, almost always resort to fundraising to implement their theme (e.g. the arts, leadership, technology, environment, etc.) because their district's per-pupil spending is inadequate. In fact, I would argue that inadequate per-pupil spending is, in part, the very reason why disgruntled and demoralized educators, parents, and community leaders seek to create these vibrant and innovative charter schools in the first place.

The elephant in the living room that everyone tiptoes around is that many states cannot by themselves raise the funds necessary to provide high-quality education. There must be a whole new approach to securing revenue as well as an increase in federal funding to do so.

We cannot demand adequate education, then fund it inadequately. Others will respond by saying, "Look how much we have already thrown at and wasted on public education." To which I say, "It hasn't been wasted; teachers have often done remarkably well with inadequate resources." Teachers have had more and more students imposed upon them in deteriorating physical classrooms and campuses in degraded neighborhoods, yet these teachers continue to battle for their students. It is society— voters, legislators, leaders—who fail our teachers and students by not providing them with decent conditions and adequate resources.

While it isn't all a matter of money, money indisputably plays a major role in the decline of public education, particularly in large urban areas. In fact, the general public is so used to poor conditions—and is itself so inured to what has been called "the bad becoming normal"—that it no longer knows what quality is. The five criteria outlined above are minimal. Yet, to achieve such minimal standards, we would have to increase spending on education substantially, increases that would simply get us to "adequacy."

I believe that the wealthiest nation in the history of the world should aspire to more than adequacy. Our goal should be to create *superior schools for all our children and youth*. Chapters 3, 4, 5, and 6 present what would be required for us to move beyond mere adequacy to excellence.

The Adequacy Quiz

Question: Which of the following are un*important and should not be funded?*

A. **The "other five solids"**—The arts, physical education, human development, environmental studies, community service.
B. **Counseling**—Family, special needs, college, vocational.
C. **After school**—Clubs, teams, arts performances, tutorials, etc.
D. **Administrative support**—Academic affairs, teacher training, curriculum issues, coordination of parent concerns, budget management, etc.
E. **Parent support systems**—parenting skills, volunteerism, parent organization.

Answer: None are un*important; all* should be funded.

Question: Who gets what? (Cost per pupil / inmate, 2004–05)

1) $2,982 2) $6,500 3) $22,000 4) $35,000+

A. Los Angeles public school _____
B. Westside private school (L.A.) _____
C. L.A. elementary parochial school _____
D. California prison system _____

Answer: A—2; B—3; C—1; D—4. Public school, $6,500; private school, $22,000; parochial school, $2, 982; prison system, $35,000+.

Question: What K–12 classroom size is best?
A. One teacher to 15–25 students
B. One teacher to 26–35 students
C. One teacher to 36–55 students

16

Answer: A (ask any teacher).

Question: How do most students flunk out?

A. Academically
B. Emotionally
C. Socially

Answer: B. (A and C are consequences of B.)

Question: Who receives "the other five solids"? (the arts, environmental studies, human development, physical education, and community service)

A. Well-to-do private schools
B. Large urban public schools

Answer: A, but not B (of course).

NOTES:

1 Peter Schrag, *Final Test* (New York: The New Press, 2003), p. 127.

2 Ibid., p. 128.

3 David J. Hoff, "Texas Judge Rules Funds Not Enough," *Education Week*, September 22, 2004, p. I,30.

4 Helen F. Ladd, Rosemary Chalk, and Janet S. Hansen, eds., *Equity and Adequacy in Education Finance* (Washington, D.C.: National Academy Press) 1999.

5 Bruce D. Baker, "The Emerging Shape of Educational Adequacy," *Journal of Education Finance,* Winter 2005, pp. 259–287.

6 Alfred A. Lindseth, "Adequacy Lawsuits: The Wrong Answer for Our Kids," *Education Week*, June 9, 2004, p. 52.

7 William G. Ouchi. *Making Schools Work. (*New York: Simon & Schuster, 2003).

8 Chris Whittle, *Crash Course: Imagining a Better Future for Public Education*, (New York: Riverhead Books, 2005).

CHAPTER 3

A Tale of Two Schools

It was the best of times
It was the worst of times.
—Charles Dickens,
A Tale of Two Cities

This chapter will focus on two schools: one private and one public. The schools' names will be withheld, though their identities may be clear to some people. This comparison reveals varying discrepancies in equity surrounding our education of America's children. What are we willing to tolerate? What are we willing and not willing to fund?

School A

School A is a private or independent school (K–12; 1,100 students, coed), more diverse than many private schools, more progressive and innovative than most schools, and located near both wealthy and low-income neighborhoods. About 30 percent are minority students, and approximately 11 percent of the $29-million operating budget ($3.3 million in 2005–06) is set aside for financial aid. (In other words, the school forgoes $3.3 million in potential tuition income in order to enroll students who could not otherwise afford to attend the school.)

Given that the school's 2005–06 operating budget was $29 million and the total enrollment was 1,145 students, the school was spending $25,327 per student. What does that per-pupil number purchase? First of all, 100 percent of students at that school attend college, year after year. It also purchases:

1. A full college preparatory curriculum;
2. Small classes (20 or fewer), with most teachers teaching only four sections;
3. A well-educated and experienced administrative team consisting of:

- ◆ a headmaster and assistant headmaster
- ◆ directors of the elementary, middle, and high schools
- ◆ an administrator assisting the elementary and middle school heads
- ◆ numerous deans at the high school level
- ◆ counselors
- ◆ an admissions office of three administrators and three staff people
- ◆ two full-time college counselors
- ◆ a nurse
- ◆ a business office of six people
- ◆ a development office of six
- ◆ a maintenance, security and facility staff of 55 people;

4. A diverse student body, funded in part by the $3.3 million financial aid budget;
5. A multifaceted, secure, attractive, well-maintained campus with a rich variety of resources;
6. A comprehensive arts department with 14 full-time and 25 part-time teachers, including majors programs for students;
7. A comprehensive environmental and outdoor education program with field trips and overnight trips to the mountains, deserts and oceans;
8. A comprehensive physical education and athletic program with 10 full-time teachers and coaches and assistant coaches for 27 teams;
9. A rich human development program attending to the emotional needs of young people and adolescents;
10. A community service program that is a graduation requirement for all students;
    (Note: Items 6 through 10 constitute what I call "the other five solids"; see Chapter 2.)
11. A rich classics program (including four years of classical Greek) and other non-conventional courses such as ethics, film criticism, and astronomy—which appeal to a wide range of student interests;
12. A diverse and substantial after-school menu of arts, athletic clubs, and activities.

Is this all necessary, one may ask, for high-quality, or even adequate, education? Yes. Every child warrants the program and resources offered by School A. The results are clear:

College attendance and graduation	100 percent
Students who say they enjoy going to school and believe their education is meaningful and engaging	100 percent
Drop-outs	0 percent
Students in gangs, prisons, etc.	0 percent

Let us now compare School B—a composite, Los Angeles Unified School District (LAUSD) middle and high school, not untypical of urban, inner-city schools across the country. I say composite because I am combining district statistics and first-hand visits to several schools to describe the typical School B.

School B

School B is a school of 3,000 to 4,000 students, receiving approximately $6,500 per pupil, spending less than one-third of what School A spends to educate each child. What does the $6,500 fund? Typically, School B will have 35 to 45 students per class. In some neighborhoods between 30 and 50 percent will drop out between grades 6–9, and fewer than 50 percent of ninth-grade students will graduate from the high school. Far fewer will attend two- or four-year colleges. The curriculum may offer the University of California A–F requirements, but with vastly reduced options compared to School A. For example, there may be a band or a chorus, but there will *not* be a string orchestra, choral groups, jazz ensembles, dance electives, chamber music groups, master classes, music theory classes (Level I–IV), a diverse list of visual arts electives, a major in music, dance, drama, or the visual arts, several drama classes— acting, mime, improvisation, technical theatre, directing, etc.—as at School A. At best, there will be a bare-bones arts program at School B, and, consequently, many potentially gifted students will never even know what their gifts are or might have been. Some of these students, having been denied a creative mode of self-expression, will find other less productive means of expression, joining gangs, becoming pregnant, engaging in drug activities, or even serving time in juvenile detention or big-time prison systems.

For example, consider these conditions at Garfield High—the school immortalized in Hollywood's 1988 *Stand and Deliver*, a film about teacher Jaime Escalante as portrayed by Edward James Olmos:

> At Garfield High, for example, nearly 60 percent of the class of 2002 had dropped out by graduation day; one in 16 students enter a four-year college, and the school is overcrowded, with its 4,800 students on staggered, shortened schedules. Some students complain that they cannot get the courses they need for admission to four-year colleges and say military recruiters come calling at the campus but not college representatives. [1]

In School B class size will be 35 (minimum) and some classes will have 45 or even 50 students or more in a class. The teacher will often have five or even six sections and will therefore be mostly a disciplinarian focusing on simple classroom control. An English teacher, for example, with a load of 175 students (5 x 35) will simply not be able to assign, evaluate, and return with comments weekly—or even monthly—essays. An English teacher at School A with a load of 80 (4 x 20) *will* be able to do so. As Jonathon Kozol states, "There is no doubt in my mind that a good teacher with 20 children is twice as good as a good teacher with 40 children." [2] Kozol's observation is not just a casual opinion; it is, in fact, supported by research. For example, the STAR project (Student Teacher Achievement Ratio) was designed to involve a broad range of schools throughout Tennessee—a diverse state. It was a four-year project, 1985–89, and reached the 'startling' conclusion that: "Teachers with a greater level of skill are better able to use the opportunities that small classes afford." [3] The STAR report also validated the efficacy of smaller classes leading to greater student achievement. The results are that School A graduates will be superbly prepared for college, while School B grads generally will not be.

School B will certainly not have an environmental–outdoor education program (headed by full-time employees). The students will not have slept under the stars, hiked in redwood forests, paddled in the gulfs of Baja California, as have students in School A. School B will not have a comprehensive community service program (a graduation requirement for all School A students). Thus, graduates or attendees of School B will leave the school not having experienced or learned directly about ecology and environmental issues; they will have no relation to the earth and little understanding of the crises facing the planet. They will also have little direct understanding of how they might serve their community in a positive way. Isn't this a loss to society?

School B will have limited outlets in varsity or junior varsity athletics, perhaps a football and/or basketball program, but certainly not tennis, golf, riding, soccer, track and cross-country, gymnastics, baseball and softball, swimming and water polo, fencing, and volleyball teams, which School A has been able to offer over the years. Consequently, while most School A students are engaged in after-school sports programs, many School B students are "on the streets," where a statistically significant percentage will be absorbed into the situations of social disorder mentioned above.

For most students, the curricular deficiencies are not as devastating as the overall oppressive atmosphere of depression and demoralization that hangs over the school. The class sizes, the filthy, dilapidated campuses, the teacher turnover and often teaching ineptitude is a clear message that "No one cares about us. We inner city kids are relegated to the bottom of the ladder, where we are meant to stay."

Is this fair? Is this acceptable to us as a society? We will return to these questions later.

Let us continue listing the many benefits of the $25,327 per pupil spending at School A compared to $6,500 at School B. School A—a private school—has racial diversity; School B— located in an ethnic-racial neighborhood predominantly Latino or Asian or African-American or white—will have less. School A's campus is well maintained, with a well-equipped gymnasium, a soccer field, swimming pool, dance studios, aesthetically pleasing landscaping, and buildings designed by leading architects. School B is undermaintained, with unimaginative box-shaped bungalows painted bilious colors, playgrounds often a mess of cracked, weed-infested asphalt, netless basketball rims long since bent down: in short, virtually unplayable. Nor are there soccer fields or tennis or volleyball courts.

School A is alive after school with clubs, intra- and extramural teams, debate teams, arts and drama productions, middle-school sports leagues, tutorial programs, community service projects, journalism and literary magazine projects, etc. At 3:15 p.m. School B will fall silent; the teachers leave and activities cease.

So when people tell you that the problem with public schools is *not* a lack of funding, I say hogwash. Spending three times as much at School A brings those students a high-quality education in an excellent facility. Spending three times less at School B brings them less than even adequate schooling. It is, significantly, a matter of spending.

Adequacy and Excellence

Often, the difference between adequacy and excellence is a matter of the quality of the people running the programs. A well-designed program implemented by a mediocre teacher or administrator will often yield a mediocre program; a barely adequate teacher may not inspire a potentially excellent class. The key is to at least offer the program. Without the program there is no possibility of excellence or even adequacy. Consequently, when we examine many inner-city schools, what we see is an absence of crucial programs that engage students and make the daily work more meaningful. All of these programs exist at school A, very few at B.

To provide our students with adequate-to-excellent schools, we would need to offer:

The Ten Solids
The five traditional academic subjects: English, history, math, science, foreign languages. The "other five solids": the arts, physical education, human development, environmental education, and community service

Counseling
Family, special needs, college and vocational

After-School Programs
Clubs, teams, arts performances, tutorials, etc.

Administrative Assistance
Academic affairs, teacher training, curriculum issues, coordination of parent concerns, compliance with state and federal mandates, budget management, etc.

Parent Support Systems
Parenting skills, volunteerism, parent organization, fundraising

These offerings need to be administered and coordinated. Each is in the best interests of every student and, by extension, of society. But they must be funded. School A funds them with private tuition dollars and fundraising; School B is not provided with enough public funds to do the job.

We have been comparing programs, curricula, and administration of two schools and examining the relationship of funding to the quality and quantity of what these schools offer. What we have not yet considered is perhaps far more important—though more difficult to measure objectively. I speak of the ambiance of the schools, the feeling of community, the morale of all involved, the overall culture.

Because it is properly funded, because it has the variety of offerings and the teaching conditions mentioned above, School A is a happy, stimulating and personal place. Teachers know their students and call them by their first names; they know something of each student's life and know when a given student needs support and friendly encouragement. In short, they have genuine close relationships with their students. Given the conditions at School B, there is far less of any of this.

NOTES:

1 Jean Merl, "Community Activists Promote Education on Eastside," *Los Angeles Times*, January 29, 2005, p. B2.

2 Lynn Olson, "Kozol Book Puts Human Face on Fiscal Inequalities," *Education Week*, Sept. 25, 1991, p.1.

3 Gary Peevely, et al. "The Relationship of Class Size Effects and Teacher Salary," *Journal of Education Finance*, summer 2005, pp. 101–109.

Interlude

"Here's one: On March 10 of this year, on page B8, with a headline that stretched across all six columns, The New York Times reported that tuition in the city's elite private schools would hit $26,000 for the coming school year—for kindergarten as well as high school. On the same page, under a two-column headline, Michael Wineraub wrote about a school in nearby Mount Vernon, the first stop out of the Bronx, with a student body that is 97 percent black. It is the poorest school in the town: nine out of ten children qualify for free lunches; one out of 10 lives in a homeless shelter. During black history month this past February, a sixth grader wanted to write a report on Langston Hughes. There were no books on Langston Hughes in the library—no books about the great poet, nor any of his poems. There is only one book in the library on Frederick Douglass. None on Rosa Parks, Josephine Baker, Leontyne Price, or other giants like them in the modern era. In fact, except for a few Newberry Award books the librarian bought with her own money, the library is mostly old books—largely from the 1950s and 60s when the school was all white. A 1960 child's primer on work begins with a youngster learning how to be a telegraph delivery boy. All the workers in the book—the dry cleaner, the deliveryman, the cleaning lady—are white. There's a 1967 book about telephones which says: "when you phone you usually dial the number. But on some new phones you can push buttons." The newest encyclopedia dates from 1991, with two volumes—"b" and "r"—missing. There is no card catalog in the library—no index cards or computer."

—Bill Moyers,
"This Is a Fight of Our Lives."
(Keynote Speech, Inequality Matters Forum, New York University, 2004)

The middle class and working poor are told that what's happening to them is the consequence of Adam Smith's 'Invisible Hand.' This is a lie. What's happening to them is the direct consequence of corporate activism, intellectual propaganda, the rise of a religious orthodoxy that in its hunger for government subsidies has made an idol of power, and a string of political decisions favoring the powerful and the privileged who bought the political system right out from under us.

—Bill Moyers,
"This Is a Fight of Our Lives."
(Keynote Speech, Inequality Matters Forum
New York University, 2004)

CHAPTER 4

Per-pupil Spending

How much inequity can we tolerate
in the world's most powerful nation?
—Adrienne Rich

I have been playing my own parlor game for the past couple of years in California. I ask educators (principals, teachers, Board of Education members, district officials, superintendents and politicians), "What do we spend per pupil in our city (or state)?" I get a different answer from everyone I speak to. In the past 12 months the answers have ranged from $4,000 to $9,800, with most of the answers clustering in the $6,500 to $7,300 range. For example, this year (2004–05) at a Los Angeles charter school where I am a trustee, our operating budget is $8,719,223; our enrollment is 1,237; thus we are spending $7,048 per pupil. The superintendent of a neighboring school district says that his operating budget is $55 million and he has 7,500 students; ergo his per pupil spending is $7,333. Other Los Angeles principals have told me they don't know their per-pupil expenditure since they have virtually no control over their budgets. In his 2003 study *Making Schools Work,* William G. Ouchi has his own take on Los Angeles public education:

> Consider these facts in the Los Angeles Unified School District as an example: the annual operating budget per student for 2001–02 was $9,889. On top of that, the district budgets $2,810 per student for school construction and renovation and $375 per student for debt service. Add it all up, and it's a total of $13,074 per student per year. By comparison, a study by the *Los Angeles Business Journal* shows that for twenty-five private schools in Los Angeles, the average annual tuition is only $7,091, and our research shows that the 298 Catholic schools in the city spend an average of $2,500 per student in elementary schools and $5,100 per student in high school. [1]

Ouchi concludes, "The problem is not that there isn't enough money in public schools." I respectfully disagree. Even if Los Angeles Unified School

District principals actually had $9,889 to spend per pupil—which *none* currently do—this is still 50 percent less than what I believe is necessary to provide high-quality schools. We might produce better test-takers at $9,889 per pupil, but we would not be able to offer comprehensive and high-quality programs.

Recent federal rules have squeezed the creative juices out of students' schooling, forcing them to spend more class time merely on test preparation and test taking. Then we wonder why we have such a dropout epidemic. The real question is, what do these students *drop in to*? At best, low-paying jobs; at worst, crime, drug use, unemployment, homelessness, and depression. So when various commentators tell us that our schools have enough funds to do the job, I must ask, "What job?" If the job is solely to raise test scores, then perhaps so. If, however, the job is to provide a high-quality education, then most of our public schools are anywhere from 50 percent to 70 percent *short* of appropriate funding.

Citizens wrestling with the issue of how the nation can possibly afford to provide a superb education to all its students may be tempted to think of the additions I am proposing to the basic curriculum solely as "frills," i.e., items which should be considered jettisonable in times of fiscal constraint, such as most states are operating under today. That attitude is precisely the opposite of what I mean, and I will offer a hypothetical example to drive home my point. What if the nation decided to embark on an important rocket-building program, deciding in advance what each rocket "should" cost. In actual fact, each rocket cost a quite a bit more than that, so that all that could be built for the money allocated was an outer shell. The result product would *look* like a rocket, but since it lacked an engine inside—the most critical component—when launched, the rocket would be a complete failure. At the risk of being heavy-handed in driving home the moral of this story: Let us note that *although a great deal of money was spent* on the fruitless rocket program, the results were not just correspondingly smaller—they were *zero*. If one fails to address the elements that are *critical* to a successful educational outcome, the inadequate and stingy amounts that have been spent are even themselves a total waste, since they do not produce positive results. When we look at our nation's dismal school results and wonder why, we need to ask ourselves whether our current educational process has managed to leave out the "engine."

When I speak of "high-quality education" I am talking about something very specific. My daughters and I have spelled out our thoughts on the ingredients of such an education at some length in two previous books, *For Mortal Stakes: Solutions for Schools and Society* [2] and *Proceed With Passion: Engaging Students in Meaningful Education.* [3] These two books discuss our belief that the nation's schools can engage students and solve many current educational dilemmas when more attention—and funding—is devoted to a comprehensive curriculum.

Typically, American educators affirm the importance of English, history, math, science and foreign languages. These are called "the basics," the "core curriculum": in fact, in many schools they are the only curriculum. Anything else is, by definition, "extracurricular," and these "extras" are often relegated to after-school programs, clubs, or electives. But I believe the "other five solids" are extremely important—perhaps even more important than the first group—to the development of a well-educated, enlightened, engaged, complete person.

These "other five solids" engage students in a process that is hands-on, experiential and personal. When taught properly, they cost as much money as the other subjects, but the rewards they bring are tremendous. From more than 40 years of experience in private and public schools, I know that these five other solids pay human dividends that are crucial both to academic success and fulfillment in life. When students are engaged in one or more of them, we see astonishing results: attendance improves, engagement in one area spills over into others, and positive self-expression reduces the need for negative forms of expression (crime, gang violence, drug use, anti-social behavior, etc.). Attendance leads to fewer drop-outs, greater college enrollment, and the like. The key is *engagement.*

Using School A as a yardstick, we see that superb schools don't just prepare students for big-stakes, single-answer, standardized tests. Of course, School A does this as well, since we have seen that 100 percent of its graduates go to college. But beyond these academic successes, superb schools like School A offer comprehensive—not token, not after-school only, not eight weeks a year or every other year—fully funded programs in the five "other solids."

The Arts

Programs in all the arts (music, drama, dance, visual arts) are the means by which students discover and express the passionate, creative sides of their personalities. What is not mentioned often enough about arts programs is that when students are engaged, via creative expression, they also acquire an invaluable sense of autonomy as well as a newfound feeling that they are masters of their educational fate. This sense of personal power then spreads to other areas of their lives. Arts programs should include the following:

- Teachers who are professional artists and performers themselves
- Four-hours-a-week, sequential, skill-building classes during school hours (just like math or English)
- A rich menu of classes in music, dance, drama, and the visual arts
- Regularly scheduled concerts, recitals, master classes, exhibits, field trips, and assemblies

Yearly per-pupil cost: $1,100

Physical Education

We have all certainly read enough lately about the huge risks to the health of our nation's youth posed by current epidemics of obesity and diseases such as Type II diabetes, all the direct result of physical inactivity. If a school only manages to offer sports to a select few (football and basketball stars) and relegates the rest of the student body to being the same kind of spectators they are when watching sports on television at home, it has failed to inculcate good health habits, which can last a lifetime. A physical education program should include the following:

- Comprehensive sports programs: intra- and extramural, lifetime sports
- Courses in nutrition, yoga, physical fitness
- Programs in sportsmanship and team play

Yearly per-pupil cost: $607

Human Development

Adolescence and pre-adolescence are times of defining and discovering oneself, exploring values and examining one's role in the community. Most people do not flunk out of life intellectually, they flunk out emotionally, yet our schools act as if the above issues were unimportant or even nonexistent. With our culture becoming increasingly materialistic, while more families are disintegrating—particularly in some areas where divorce and marriage have a 1:1 ratio—we cannot assume that our cultures or families will teach the necessary life skills. If schools do not, we can be sure many children will not only be left behind, they will also be bereft of any achievement or hope. Human development programs should include the following:

- Programs in sex education, drug education, relationships, self-awareness
- One-hour-a-week sessions in which students can discuss their life issues with trained facilitators
- Retreats: time for self-reflection and community building

Yearly per-pupil cost: $417

Environmental Education

It is crucial to the future of our nation that students become aware of the necessity of becoming responsible stewards of the environment. The awareness fostered by environmental education programs that actually take place in wilderness areas is especially valuable to low-income minority students, whose families may not have been able to send them to camp or take them on the kinds of outdoor-oriented vacations that middle-class families take for granted. If a student has never encountered the wild environment, it goes without saying he or she will have no personal stake in its protection when he or she becomes an adult. An environmental education program should include the following:

- Classes and units at all grade levels
- Overnight camping, backpacking, kayaking, trips to the mountains, oceans, deserts
- Guest lectures, conferences, and workshops

Yearly per-pupil cost: $410

Community Service

Our nation faces a collection of social ills that would be entirely intractable if it weren't for the altruistic participation of ordinary citizens, whether in faith-based groups or secular charitable organizations. Again, a student who has never been exposed to the requirement to perform community service in order to graduate will be less likely to see the need to volunteer his or her charitable time in adulthood. A community service program should include the following:

- Required for graduation
- Weekly seminars, guest speakers
- Placements for field experience in senior homes, Head Start centers, soup kitchens, and the like

Yearly per-pupil cost: $140.

We will have superior schools when the following criteria can be met:

- The five other solids are woven into the daily and weekly life of each student.
- All classes are small, individualized and taught by full-time credentialed and/or degreed teachers with knowledge of and a passion for their subjects.
- The campus is attractive, inviting, well-maintained, and secure.
- There is comprehensive counseling, and an efficient, fully staffed administration.
- There are interesting and engaging activities, field trips and assemblies.

When these ingredients are present, *then* we will have superior schools. We cannot refuse to pay for this standard of quality and then delude ourselves into believing that funding is not a major issue.

NOTES:

1 William G. Ouchi, *Making Schools Work* (New York: Simon & Schuster, 2003), p.10.

2 Paul and Anna Cummins, *For Mortal Stakes: Solutions for Schools and Society* (New York: Peter Lang, 1998).

3 Paul, Anna, and Emily Cummins, *Proceed with Passion: Engaging Students in Meaningful Education* (Los Angeles: Red Hen Press, 2004).

CHAPTER 5

Throwing Away Whole
Generations of Students

*Surely there is enough for everyone within this country.
It is a tragedy that these good things are not widely
shared. All our children ought to be allowed a stake in
the enormous richness of America. Whether they were born
to poor white Appalachians or to wealthy Texans, to poor
black people in the Bronx or to rich people in Manhasset or
Winnetka, they are all quite wonderful and innocent when
they are small. We soil them needlessly.*

—Jonathan Kozol,
Savage Inequalities

This chapter specifically concerns segments of our young population that our society seems to have written off as unreachable and ineducable. Its aim is to demonstrate the positive—some have even said unbelievable—results that can be produced when a different approach to the problem is applied.

Ethnic Minorities

The principal of a public inner-city school tells me that typically his school begins with 1,800 ninth graders. At the end of the twelfth grade fewer than 900 graduate. Of the 900, approximately 300 ask for college scholarship forms. He estimates (he doesn't have the staff to track them) that 10 percent actually fill out the forms, are accepted by a college and then enroll. Hence about 30 of the original 1,800 go on to college. And as we saw earlier at Garfield High, the school of *Stand and Deliver* fame, only one in sixteen students enters a four-year college.

Across the country in New York it is much the same: "Just 18 percent of all students graduate with a Regents diploma, which is the diploma required for admission to a four year college. Only 9.4 percent of African American students get a Regents diploma." [1]

The others? Some will "make it" against all odds. But many will drop out into a society that will offer them few possibilities without a proper education. Many will join the various statistically disastrous categories: imprisoned, unemployed, homeless, welfare dependent, teen pregnant, or drug addicted. Others will join groups for which we have no statistics: depressed drifters, petty criminals from the underclass, and mentally disturbed homeless people and occasional shelter dwellers.

In addition to the drop-out crisis, we find that minority students are increasingly relegated to segregated schools. These schools are not only separate, they are—as Brown vs. Board of Education ruled in 1954—*unequal,* A recent (January '06) report from Harvard University reported findings revealing that the Brown vs. Board of Education Supreme Court decision ordering *de*segregation of American schools has been steadily eroded in the past thirty years and affects mostly African-Americans and Latinos. A co-author of the report, Gary Orfield, writes that "Our nation is risking its future when it confines its growing populations to separate and unequal schools." Orfield's co-author Chung Mei Lee reiterates: "Students who attend segregated schools will become increasingly ill-prepared to participate in a diverse society." [2]

The Harvard Report is validated by Jonathan Kozol in his new book, dramatically titled *The Shame of the Nation: The Restoration of Apartheid Schooling in America.* Kozol's travels across America to write this book confirm what I have seen in schools across Los Angeles: School after school in low-income neighborhoods are virtually all black and Latino. Few whites – in some schools, none. The Harvard Project finds that "despite an increase in diversity [in America's schools], white students remain the most isolated group." The whites, however, are isolated in better funded schools; their isolation is generally not deprivation.

Although it seems as if such doleful statistics on the plight of minority student populations have always been with us and therefore must represent a chronic problem that will exist no matter how much money is thrown at the problem, I can state with confidence that things don't have to be this way.

When colleagues and I founded Crossroads School in 1971–72, we pledged to dedicate 10 percent of the school's total budget to scholarships for minority students. (Our first budget was $45,000, which meant that the scholarship amount was $4,500.) At that time, this decision was a bold move: the average percentage of minority-student aid at Los Angeles-area private schools was more like half that. Today, ('05-06) Crossroads has grown and prospered, and its yearly operating budget is $29 million, which means that Crossroads can offer $3.3 million a year in minority and low-income scholarships.

But, we told ourselves, even that apparently generous amount of scholarship aid was insufficient. What if we took the truly radical step of starting a high-quality private school that devoted 40 percent of its tuition income to minority and low-income scholarships? We acknowledged that our plan entailed asking well-to-do parents to subsidize the education of minority and low-income students, but we reasoned that if the education we provided was of genuine high quality, parents of means would gravitate to the school out of their own family self-interest. And so New Roads School was born. Today it offers financial aid to almost 60 percent of the students and more than 50% of the school is non-white. It is one of the few truly integrated schools in the nation.

Foster Children

Statistically we know that certain groups of children who receive inferior educations are destined to fill the ranks of the above categories disproportionately. For example, foster children are a dismal indictment of our society and its treatment of children. Of the more than half a million children in America who live with foster families, most are children of color and reside in urban areas. Nearly all have suffered traumatic experiences, and many have been moved from home to home. Consequently, these children are in dire need of the quality of education that students receive in School A. Yet just the opposite occurs: they are often shuffled from one inadequate school to another. Meanwhile, wealthy children from intact families receive the services that these foster children desperately need and are denied. School B cannot provide the services they need because of funding shortfalls.

The net result is that foster children often drift from one underfunded school to the next. To give examples from Los Angeles County (which contains more than 50,000 foster youth): [3]

- ◆ 30 percent of foster youth function below grade average;
- ◆ 83 percent of foster youth will be held back by third grade;

- 46 percent of foster youth do not complete high school;
- 50 percent of emancipated foster youth are unemployed;
- 25 percent of foster youth will be incarcerated within four years of care;
- 60 percent of young women are pregnant within four years of being emancipated;
- 15 percent of foster youth enroll in college;
- One percent of foster children will graduate from college.

At first glance, the problems foster children face may seem insurmountable. They are not. A high-quality education can make all the difference. I learned this firsthand, almost inadvertently. Four years ago I received an offer to place three fully funded foster children in New Roads School. A patron—Peter Morton—wanted to do something for foster children and approached a social worker friend, Deanne Sharton. We suggested providing five foster children with full tuition to high-quality private schools. David Bryan, our school's head, said "great," and we enrolled three. I asked two other school heads to take the other two and they said "yes."

One of the three at New Roads had been to 16 schools before coming to us in the tenth grade. Sixteen schools! Needless to say, her sense of security and self-esteem were severely compromised. But attending a school like New Roads changed her life. She stayed for all three years (grades 10 through 12), graduated, and went on to college. At New Roads, her teachers knew her by name, knew her history, and were sensitive to her needs. She was for the first time exposed to the arts—which she loved. She was enrolled in small classes with other motivated and college-bound students. The atmosphere affected her immediately and stabilized her life.

This example gave me an idea: why not place other foster children in high-quality private schools? Remember the per-pupil spending in all of these independent schools is two or three times greater than the local public schools. Consequently, the students receive *all* or *most* of the services that, I believe, adequate to superior schools should offer. So our foundation, New Visions Foundation, launched a program we called Center for Educational Opportunities (CEO), and in our first year we added four students to the original five. Now we had nine students placed. All stayed at their schools and all did reasonably well.

The second year we placed 18, the third year 47, and now (2005–06) we have 66 students placed. Seven have graduated and all seven are attending college—including colleges such as M.I.T., Tufts, and Brown. Furthermore, once we place a student in a quality school, almost all of them stay at that school. This kind of stability astounds people in the foster world. What we have discovered, I believe, is that placement in a high-quality school not only stabilizes these students' lives, but also inspires them to high achievement and to set new goals for their future.

Again, we see the critical issue of funding. These students can now succeed because they attend adequately funded—and hence adequately functioning—schools. It isn't only funding that matters, but without proper funding little can be done—and then, only in the *extra*ordinary schools.

If we want to rescue our society from staggering costs of crime, prisons, drug use and drug rehabilitation, homelessness, unemployment, teen pregnancies, and the like, we would do well to fund our schools properly. As our small foster program has shown, investing in education is the best preventive of future social ills and their concomitant costs. A sum of $25,000 per pupil makes much better fiscal sense than $37,000 per prisoner.

Youthful Prisoners

Another arena in which we blatantly squander lives and dollars is our system of juvenile incarceration in many states. I stumbled upon or, more accurately, was led into this arena by two dedicated women who asked for my assessment of one of Los Angeles' nineteen juvenile camp schools, Camp Gonzales. I visited the camp in 1992 and observed that it had three problems: one, it didn't assess the students' interests, inclinations, and goals upon entry; two, it therefore could not educate, since it could not build upon what it didn't know about its students; three, it didn't place students in new or improved situations when they were released. Hence they inevitably returned to their neighborhoods, rejoined gangs and got in trouble again, either returning to the same or a different lock-up camp school or "graduating" into the adult prison system. Nationally there is about an 83 percent juvenile recidivism rate, and Camp Gonzales' rate was probably about that. I say "probably" because it is difficult to know any real statistics, since the county and probation departments conduct no longitudinal studies.

So my overall assessment was an outsider's common-sense view that the existing punitive, non-individualized programs for these juveniles were simply not working. My two compatriots, Carol Biondi and Jo Kaplan, initiated a process to secure a contract for my organization to address all three shortcomings.

We are now (2006) in our fourth year of providing an assessment, curriculum enrichment, and placement program at Camp Gonzales. A director and three full-time placement employees have secured placements for more than 80 juveniles in community colleges, private high schools, the Job Corps, Los Angeles Conservation Corps, private boarding high schools and one community college boarding school. Two students, I should add, were shot and killed in gang-related incidents one week before we could get them to their job interviews. A third student whom we had placed in a state college with a boarding school was killed in 2005 when he came home for summer vacation. In some cases placement is literally a life and death issue.

If the recidivism rate of 80 percent is accurate, our program is enormously cost effective. Each prisoner costs the state of California approximately $37,000 per year, not to mention hundreds of thousands of dollars over their prison "careers." Here is another case in which public funds can take statistically doomed youth and redirect their lives. Our program serves about 200 juveniles per year with a total budget of $367,000. It is a bargain to taxpayers and society at large.

A high percentage of the students whom we cannot place—because of a lack of funding—are doomed to the statistical waste bin mentioned earlier. It is difficult to avoid seeing a racist picture in all this, for a disproportionately high number of incarcerated youth are African-American and Latino, as they are in the larger prison systems. If we are to become a truly just society, we will find the funds to improve our juvenile and adult justice systems; in addition to our foster and other at-risk students. These conditions are a deep wound afflicting our country.

I think it bears repeating: A toxic and self-defeating mindset is currently at work in our nation. Collectively, as a society, we have become utterly numbed to the enormous social costs we are being forced to shoulder as an inevitable outcome of our stinginess in funding public education. Incredibly, we seem to believe that there is no escape from these dire consequences, while we are blind to the common-sense measures that would go a long way toward preventing them entirely.

NOTES:

1 Bob Herbert, "Education's Collateral Damage," *New York Times,* 7-21-05, p. A 27.

2 www.civilrightsproject.harvard.edu/news/pressreleases/deseg06.php.

3 Little Hoover Commission Report, *Still in Our Hands: A Review of Efforts to Reform Foster Care in California,* February 2003; *Foster Care Fundamentals, L.A. Educational Summit on Needs and Challenges Facing Foster Youth, A Review of Emancipation Services,* Los Angeles County Emancipation Program Final Report, July 2003.

Interlude

R. is a superb, award-wining fifth grade teacher in a low-income school. His students are Latino and Asian, and most come from non-English-speaking families. His accomplishments are by now well known: his students read 10 to 12 paperback novels a year (which he pays for); they read *and* perform an entire Shakespeare play every year (which he funds); they travel to Ashland, Oregon, and Utah (and once to London) for Shakespeare festivals—for which he raises the funds. His students meet him when they are off-track; they arrive at school at 6:30 a.m. and go home at 5:00 p.m. Over his door there is a sign: "There Are No Short-cuts." His students are engaged, they love learning, and they are determined to achieve and to go to college.

But R. cannot do what he does on $6,500 per pupil. He has set up his own 501(c)3 nonprofit organization, and he raises funds for his one fifth grade class. Is this a replicable model? No. Few teachers could do what R. does. He raises more than $4,500 extra per pupil! As a result, R's kids receive what few others in the system receive. R. has to go outside the system to produce quality. $6,500 per pupil doesn't work. He makes it work at $11,000 per pupil. And the $11,000 doesn't factor in all the extra time he *donates* to his students; he doesn't even allot himself *any* money from his fundraising; it all goes to the students. It is a truly extraordinary situation.

Of course, that is the point: it is *EXTRA*-ordinary in public schools. Only a handful of children get R.; the others get a bare-bones program of $6,500 per pupil. It need not be so.

> *The test of our progress is not whether we add more*
> *to the abundance of those who have much; it is*
> *whether we provide enough for those who have too little.*
> —Franklin D. Rosevelt, 1937

CHAPTER 6

Teachers' Salaries: Attracting the Best

The trouble with this restaurant is that the
food is lousy and the portions are too small.
—Yogi Berra

I doubt if I have ever heard a politician speak of education without emphasizing the importance of teachers in our society. Yet when it comes to paying our teachers adequate or even generous salaries, suddenly legislatures and taxpayers argue that we don't have the money or resources. Of course, we *do* have the funds; we simply lack the will and the priorities. That contention is the essence of this book.

According to a June 2003 report by the Bureau of Labor Statistics, in 2002 the average salary of lawyers was $90,875 and engineers $68,759, while that of teachers averaged $51,617 (or approximately $66,000 adjusted for twelve-month employment). [1] According to a 2004 study by the Economic Policy Institute, "Teachers' wages have slipped by nearly 15 percent since 1993 and 12 percent since 1983, after adjusting for inflation. In 2003, teachers earned an average of $833 in gross pay a week, compared with $1,078 for other college graduates." [2] Senator Jim Jeffords (formerly Republican, now Independent) points out that one-third of all seniors graduating from institutes of higher education leave with more than $20,000 of debt. Jeffords then trenchantly adds: "How many graduates leaving college with at least a $20,000 debt can afford to sign up for a teaching job that pays, on average, a beginning salary between $25,000 and $35,000?" [3] The question virtually answers itself.

I believe we have grown so accustomed to thinking of educational reform in a context of limited revenue or cutting expenses and services that actually increasing salaries for our beleaguered teachers is not even on the national radar screen. Low wages for teachers have seemingly become ingrained in our culture.

Granted, for much of our nation's history the social contract with teachers to pay them chronically low wages was not as reprehensible a

45

social choice as it is today. During the nineteenth and the early twentieth centuries many of the nation's teachers were young unmarried women, who may have entered teaching as a stopgap measure before entering into marriage and raising a family. (Women teachers were uniformly unmarried women, since most school districts, exhibiting a strange Puritanical streak, actually barred married women from classroom teaching.) Such young unmarried ladies were thought to have lower living expenses than men trying to raise a family, and this idea was also thought to be true of women teachers who never married, and who remained in the teaching profession as spinsters.

However, the world has changed beyond recognition since those early days of the teaching profession. While the gender ratio in teaching has changed, there are still many women teachers, although today they could easily be the sole wage earners for their families, finding life extremely difficult trying to survive on a minimum pay scale. If this were not enough cause for concern, we find also that "the least qualified and thus the lowest paid teachers tend to be concentrated in the schools serving the poorest children." [4] The lack of funding for poor districts reveals a vicious circle: class size is higher than in wealthier districts, and poor teaching conditions make it difficult to recruit high-quality teachers. Good teachers, not surprisingly, want to be able to teach their subjects. In overcrowded classrooms, they cannot teach effectively. Therefore, they gravitate towards districts where they *can* teach. Generally these are wealthier districts. Consequently, the poorer districts are often forced to recruit less qualified teachers for the students who most need superb teachers. In addition, in these more difficult districts and schools, the teacher turnover rate is huge. For example, a recent report entitled "Is There Really a Teacher Shortage?" [5] alleged that 40 to 50 percent or more of new teachers leave the profession during their first five years. Students on the least-level playing fields are subjected to the least qualified teachers and the greatest turnover and lack of consistency of faculty support. Is it any wonder that it is so difficult to raise performance scores in low-income-area schools?

One way to break this vicious circle would be to pay teachers generous and attractive salaries at all levels, but certainly pay more in "combat zones." However, whenever one suggests raising teachers' salaries as a significant solution, one is likely to encounter the contrarians' conservative position that the problems with schools lie primarily in areas such as inadequate curricula, the need for testing and accountability, swollen educational bureaucracies, and the like. Rarely is funding the issue. "But," as Peter Schrag counters in his excellent and comprehensive book, *Final Test:* "When a school has a string of [substitute teachers], no books to give to the kids for homework, and constant shifting of classes and bodies, when it's bereft of functioning labs and counselors to deal with student crises, and when for one of many reasons the leaky roof doesn't get fixed, the chances of teaching anything will go down fast." [6]

The chances of hiring and retaining high-quality teachers also go down fast. More and more we find teachers teaching for one or two or three years and then just leaving the field. The pay is simply not enough to compensate for the compromised teaching conditions, the frustrations, and the heartbreak. Furthermore, in many cities, someone going into teaching today is forgoing the possibility of ever owning his or her own home for the simple reason that the cost of housing in urban areas has increased at a faster rate than teachers' salaries. If the nation as a whole owes a debt to its dedicated but beleaguered teachers, surely it would be possible to institute a federal low-interest-loan program to help teachers with the purchase of a home they might otherwise never be able to afford.

I have rarely talked to any concerned educator, politician, or citizen who doesn't deplore the generally low salaries of teachers. Yet few people then move on to the logical solution: Raise public revenue and pay them better! We all observe the phenomenon of state and federal legislators rewarding themselves with raises and higher salaries—which, of course, must be covered by increased public revenue—i.e., taxes. Why then do we not do the same for our teachers?

Senator Jim Jeffords writes: "I don't believe the solution to this dilemma is that complicated. *The federal government must increase its role in funding public education.*" Jeffords explains further:

In the late 1940s, with the creation of the G.I. Bill, the percentage of the total federal budget dedicated to education was 10.7 percent. Some sixty years later, that amount—which covers funding for elementary, secondary, and higher education—has dwindled to slightly less than three percent. The federal government must reach back into history and return to dedicating ten percent of the total federal budget to education. [7]

47

If our legislators are worth $158,000 a year, then should not our children's and young people's teachers be of equal value? If we truly wish to have superb schools, we must attract the best and brightest college graduates to the teaching profession. To do this, we need to pay them salaries commensurate with our rhetoric of the importance of teaching.

In his book *The $100,000 Teacher* [8] Brian Crosby suggests a specific salary number. Recently, a friend of mine, a superior 14-year veteran teacher (who has won many awards), told me a law firm offered his daughter a starting salary three times greater than his salary in a Los Angeles public school. He was making $40,000 after 14 years of teaching; she was offered $120,000. What does this say about our national priorities? Why isn't the teacher worth $100,000+? Why aren't we willing to find the funds? As Parts II, III, and IV of this book point out, the funds are available. It is a gross injustice to all children, those charged with their education, and to society to undervalue and underpay our teachers.

NOTES:

1 Martin Sullivan, "US Multinationals Profit from Tax Havens," *Tax Notes,* October, 2004.

2 Kathleen Kennedy Manzo, "Study Finds Teachers Are Losing Ground on Salary Front," *Education Week*, September 1, 2004, p. 12.

3 Quoted in Carl Glickman, *Letters to the Next President* (New York: Teachers College Press, Columbia University, 2004), p. 43.

4 Peter Schrag, *Final Test: The Battle for Adequacy in America's Schools.* (New York: The New Press. 2003), p. 3.

5 Carol Jago, "Giving Teachers a Helping Hand," *Los Angeles Times,* February 5, 2005, p. B19.

6 Schrag, op. cit., p. 56.

7 Glickman, op. cit., p.43.

8 Brian Crosby, *The $100,000 Teacher.* (Sterling, Virginia: Capital Books, 2001).

CHAPTER 7

Reform: Is Money All We Need?

For the task of preventing the new
generation from changing in any
deed or significant way is precisely
what most societies require of
their educators.

—George B. Leonard,
Education and Ecstasy

Many allege that more money will not help us solve our educational problems. I agree that more money by itself is not sufficient. But often people say that more money won't help as a prelude to arguing that we *do* have enough money to fund our schools adequately, and that the real problems are structural and systemic. That contention is only a half-truth. The reality encompasses both premises:

1. We do not fund our schools and our teachers at acceptable levels
2. We need to make structural and systemic changes in how we deliver education and how we spend the funds allocated to it.

We need additional funding AND we need to restructure and make systemic changes in public education. What structural and systemic changes are needed? Three major changes would dramatically enhance the quality of education in America:

1. Site-based management and budgetary autonomy
2. Smaller schools/smaller class size
3. Increased public–private partnerships

In fact, implementing all three of these principles is crucial if we wish to improve the quality of our schools.

For the past fourteen years I have been working with public school principals, through a private foundation, to bring arts programs to public schools. While I have been impressed with the principals' dedication and competence, I have also been amazed at the amount of paperwork imposed upon them by local, district, state, and federal regulations.

They drown in paperwork. Consequently, they are far less able to lead, visit classes, and create new programs. Many have virtually no discretionary spending funds. And while each school has its own separate needs, neighborhood issues, and student demographics, principals lack the flexibility and financial wherewithal to take advantage of opportunities or to implement badly needed arts programs. Often they are required to spend funds on projects they *don't* need while lacking funds for ones they *do* need.

One principal told me he does not know what his per-pupil spending is, and that he has no control over the distribution of funds for his school. Remember Chapter 4, where School A's headmaster designs and implements his entire budget. After paying the fixed mortgage and rental fees, he hires and fires, determines which faculty positions to add or delete, implements new programs and deletes old ones, and makes all major decisions regarding short- and long-term budget planning. Public school principals have few of these powers. Furthermore, the headmaster of School A can respond to immediate needs with immediate spending from a variety of discretionary accounts. In short, he can truly lead, whereas public-school principals' leadership capabilities are severely restricted by their lack of financial control.

Remember my argument in Chapter 3 that for a school to be truly relevant to its students, it must provide them with autonomy in their learning lives and help them discover personal *meaning* in what they are being taught. If a school can't provide meaning, any kind of educational effort it makes will be fruitless and alienating to students. It only takes a bit of thinking to realize that the same is true of the other side of the school equation: that is, among teachers and administrators. If these professionals are made to feel that they are helpless and that they lack individual autonomy in their careers, they will find it very hard not to feel alienated and apathetic as they do their daily work, and this apathy will be communicated all too readily to their students.

What are the solutions? For one, it would be desirable to transfer as much as possible of the central district bureaucracy funds to the principals on each campus. This would mean streamlining the central bureaucracy. I say "streamlining," but not eliminating. It would be self-defeating to give principals more funds, then make it necessary for them to hire more on-site administrators to do all the necessary bookkeeping, special education paperwork, payrolls, insurance forms, compliance with state and federal mandates, and the like. The bogeyman cited by many educational critics is big bureaucracy. But we must not forget that when a society chooses to educate *all* its children, innumerable administrative tasks must be performed. Many so-called bureaucrats are skilled professionals doing excellent and necessary work. So while transferring funds from downtown to each public school site is an important first step, as William Ouchi argues in *Making Schools Work*, it alone will not solve the other problems: funding comprehensive curricula and renovating campuses. Site-based management will, however, improve the efficiency with which additional funds are delivered and spent.

Many people have already written about a second desirable systemic change; the first of these was perhaps E. F. Schumacher in his 1975 book *Small is Beautiful.* [1] Actually, the tension between centralization and decentralization has been with us for quite a while. One even detects a pendulum effect beginning with the 19th century expansion of local public schools across the country to several pendulum swings during the 20th century. For example, books like James Bryant Conant's *The American High School Today* [2] and Myron Lieberman's *Future of American Education* [3] argued that greater district consolidation, with big schools absorbing several smaller schools, would provide greater curricular opportunities and more efficient management. For a while liberals agreed that small schools represented racist, bigoted, narrow-minded thinking and that a more centralized, cosmopolitan bureaucracy could mandate segregation and inefficiency out of existence.

Then the pendulum swung again as others on the left, like Jonathan Kozol, Herbert Kohl, Peter Schrag, and David Rogers, "drawing on their personal experiences teaching in inner-city schools," described "how established bureaucratic structures isolated urban school officials from the communities they were supposed to serve and frustrated nearly every attempt at curricular or pedagogic reform." [4]

Critics of centralization came later from the political right as writers like Milton Friedman, John Chubb and Terry Moe argued for greater freedom and privatization in education. They believe the market, by means of instruments such as vouchers, would create competition and hence greater quality.

And so the pendulum swings and thinkers on both sides have themselves shifted positions. I believe that either–or solutions are too simplistic to solve our educational problems. Some jobs can be done more efficiently "downtown" and some restrictions and standards (i.e., meeting the needs of special-education children, prohibiting racial discrimination, allocating equitable spending) must be centrally mandated for all schools. With respect to delivering the curriculum, however, smaller is usually better.

Small grade-level enrollments, creating small learning communities in which teachers and administrators can engage with students individually, are almost impossible in a high school of 4,000 students. Education at its best is personal. Teachers and students flourish when they are in relationships that have been established within a collegial, personalized atmosphere. In short, the entire campus needs to offer a sense of community. Beyond a certain size (300–700), achieving this goal is no longer possible.

In order to bring to our students the full set of possibilities available to them in a democratic society, and the sense of what they can make out of their lives, we need to forge partnerships between the public and the private sector. These partnerships, which are often surprisingly cost-effective, allow mentors, artists, businesspeople, senior citizens, and other professionals to share their passions and skills with schools and students in a host of programs. For example, in large urban areas there are many grassroots organizations in drama, music, visual arts, dance, film, and creative writing, each headed up by talented individuals committed to their field. They bring to schools a whole new dimension: not only do they teach students the basics of their particular art form, but they also model their commitment and plant seeds in students' minds and souls for future college majors or careers. Bringing such groups to a campus can have a transformative effect both for individual students and for the school itself.

In 1990, I created the Crossroads Community Foundation, now named P.S. Arts. We raise funds to restore the arts to public schools where budget cuts have vastly reduced or even eliminated them. We provide 26 schools with classes in music, art, dance, and drama. We fully fund the arts teachers' salaries, summer training courses, workshops and conferences, assemblies and field trips for the students, and workshops for the classroom teachers. We now raise $3 million a year and serve 14,000 children a week in courses that are sequential and skill-building. Our courses are offered at every grade level during the school day; they are not *extra*curricular, brief exposures, or after-school-only activities. As a result of this public–private collaboration, the morale at many schools has improved, corridors are filled with student art, graduations feature children playing instruments, and parents attend arts events in large numbers. Success stories of individual students coming alive abound and give heartwarming validation to the impact of the arts on students' lives. At one particular charter school I helped to launch, we have a series of collaborations not only with P.S. Arts, but also with a dance academy (the Gabriella Axelrad Foundation) and a keyboard music/math program (M.I.N.D. Institute). These three collaborations enrich everyone's lives and are administered far more effectively by their own staff teams than if the schools tried to emulate their efforts.

Returning to the question raised in this chapter: "Is money enough?" The answer demands an emphatic repetition of "No, it isn't enough." Structural and systemic changes are needed in addition. But the key to the answer is *in addition*. Our current per-pupil spending across the nation is *not* enough to provide the programs and reforms needed for superb schools. Increased spending coupled with improved structures and systems will, however, yield wonderful results. The morass of public education is so enormous and so persistent that most Americans despair that change is impossible. Yet when you see quality schools—both public and private, some struggling against seemingly insurmountable odds—you know it is possible. We need to drastically improve the odds and make it not only a possibility, but a reality, for all our children to have adequately funded, intelligently administered schools.

Now we proceed to the question "Where will the funding come from?"

NOTES:

1 E. F. Schumacher, *Small Is Beautiful* (New York: Perennial/Harper & Row, 1975).

2 James Bryant Conant, *The American High School Today.* (New York: A Signet Book, 1961).

3 Myron Lieberman, *Future of Public Education.* (Chicago, IL: University of Chicago Press, 1962).

4 Harvey Kantor and Robert Lowe, "Bureaucracy Left and Right: Thinking About the One Best System," in *Reconstructing the Common Good in Education*, ed. Larry Cuban and Dorothy Shipps (Stanford, California: Stanford University Press, 2000).

Part II

Correcting Existing Systems:
The Corporations

*A democratic society makes choices and
those choices will reflect what its people
truly value. And every society, even a
very rich one, has to live with the consequences
wise or foolish.*

—William Greider,
One World, Ready or Not

Preface

Of the eleven most developed countries in the world, the
United States is the most unequal society: Both in income
and wealth, the U.S. ranked 11th out of eleven.

—The Luxembourg Income Study (1995)

The money that would give us superb American schools *is* available: it simply has been allocated to other less admirable and productive purposes.

In the chapters that follow, I have a great deal to say about the corporate and individual greed that is siphoning away the money that we need to make our schools the envy of the world. This greed is firmly—not to mention permanently—entrenched in our society, particularly so because of the cozy relationship between elected officials and the donations made to them by the corporate beneficiaries of a variety of tax exemptions and loopholes.

As I was writing this book, I realized with a certain sense of futility that at this moment apparently *no* segment of our society could be made to care about this problem:

- The rich obviously have no motive to want the status quo to change, since they benefit from things the way they are now.
- Many members of the middle class are currently distracted by ceaseless shopping for ever more frivolous and expensive consumer goods, nonstop televised sports, and video games. Furthermore, they have to work harder and harder—often with both husband and wife working—just to maintain a precarious balance.
- After decades of buffeting, the poor feel despair and alienation from the political process, and lack the economic muscle of the wealthy to influence lawmakers in their favor.

Given these melancholy circumstances—shouting about a critical American problem when no one seems to want to listen or take it seriously—I would probably be unwilling even to consider writing this book if it weren't for two rock-solid and fundamental convictions of mine:

- ◆ There is a fundamental decency and sense of justice in the American psyche, and in the long run these qualities lead Americans to sense and to do the right thing, even (if necessary) repudiating venal and corrupt political leadership.

- ◆ In the long run—sometimes the *very* long run—corporate and legislative wrongdoing is inevitably exposed to the glare of public attention, most often by crusading reporters. At that moment the public suddenly becomes galvanized and demands reform. (Does anyone remember when the words Enron, Global Crossing, and Tyco stood for respected members of the business community? No longer: in the public mind they now represent unvarnished greed and culpability.) I still hold onto the hope that something similar could happen to redress the grievous injustices and misallocation of resources described in Part II, which follows.

Critical moments in history can, it seems, only be understood backward: with the perspective of history, we can look back at a former era and ask, Why couldn't those people see what was coming? All the hints were there, to be grasped and understood—it's just that no one seemed to be paying attention at the time. George Santayana once famously wrote, "Those who cannot remember history are condemned to repeat it." If you believe we Americans are entirely too smart to fall into the trap of being forced to repeat history, consider only one word: Vietnam.

We are at a similarly critical juncture right at this moment in history. *New York Times* columnist Thomas Friedman refers to this historical moment over and over as an "inflection point," by which he means the inevitable point on any graph of exponential growth in which the trend line begins to move sharply upward. India and China, which have invested much more of their respective gross domestic product in education than has the U.S., are now competing for our best "knowledge worker" jobs, and this competition will only intensify in the decades ahead.

Friedman has been writing passionately for years on the coming challenges and threats of globalization—what he calls the "flattening of the world"—first with his 2000 book, *The Lexus and the Olive Tree*, and now with his most recent book, *The World Is Flat: A Brief History of the 21st Century* (2005). Friedman tells us that if we don't wake up to the need to educate our children rigorously and optimally, we will find ourselves slipping to the status of a second-rate power in the fairly near future.

Bill Gates is one of the richest men in the world, whose fortune was built by the efforts of bright, highly educated employees working in a collegial atmosphere. If Bill Gates is telling his fellow citizens that the quality of American education is so important that they should now consider it Job # 1, shouldn't all of us look up from our momentary distractions and listen up? It could be that our entire way of life is at stake.

> *A government which robs Peter to pay Paul can always depend on the support of Paul.*
> —George Bernard Shaw

CHAPTER 8

Fairness, Justice, and
Progressive Corporate Taxes

*Anybody has the right to evade taxes
if he can get away with it. No citizen
has a moral obligation to assist in
maintaining the government.*

—J. Pierpont Morgan

Corporate Subsidies

It should be simple: the more profit a company shows, the more taxes it should pay. After all, no corporation—and no individual for that matter—operates in a vacuum. Both society and government make possible the accumulation of wealth. A trucking company, for example, is dependent on highways that it neither built nor maintains. According to a 1996 report from the CATO Institute, "businesses in America receive direct tax subsidies of more than $75 billion annually. That equates to every household in America paying a $750 annual subsidy to corporations." [1] In 1998, seven of America's 82 largest corporations paid "less than zero in federal income taxes" (they received rebates instead) and "44 of the 82 didn't pay the standard federal corporate income tax rate of 35 percent." [2] An April 2004 General Accounting Office report indicates that more than 60 percent of U.S. corporations didn't pay *any* federal income taxes for 1996 through 2000. [3] Enron, for example, paid *no* federal income tax in four of the five years between 1996 and 2000. [4] In addition, in September of 2004, Citizens for Tax Justice examined 275 of the largest and ***most profitable*** *Fortune 500* companies and discovered that "almost a third managed to pay nothing in federal income taxes in at least one of the first three years of the Bush administration. Over that period, the 275 companies reported $1.1 trillion in pretax U.S. profits to their shareholders, but told the IRS that they'd made less than half of that." [5] These facts are, quite simply, outrageous.

Meanwhile, state and public education systems across the nation continue cutting services for poor children. Governments complain that they just do not have enough funds to comply with various court mandates to provide an adequate education for K–12 students. The money is available; it is simply being hoarded by an elite who seem to believe their excessive lifestyle trumps children's rights to a decent education.

Today, 51 of the world's 100 largest economies are corporations and the other 49 are nation-states. As INFACT reports, "Policies affecting the health and well-being of people around the world are developed in corporate boardrooms and in global institutions unaccountable to the public." In fact, the corporate board members often have little regard for the public, and their accounting systems are designed to cheat citizens out of services that taxes would otherwise support. The dramatic reduction of corporate taxation has somehow escaped public awareness and the media's attention. In the 1950s, corporate taxes provided more than 27 percent of federal revenues. By the 1990s, they accounted for just over 10 percent. As Charles Lewis and Bill Allison point out in *The Cheating of America*, "As the corporate tax base shrank, that burden was shifted to individuals." [6]

Percent of Federal Revenue 1960		2005
Payroll Taxes	15.9 %	35.6 %
Corporate Taxes	27 %	10 %

Lewis and Allison add, "The declining tax rate for corporations doesn't tell the whole story. The Internal Revenue Code grants them generous deductions that ordinary taxpayers can only dream of." [7] As a percentage of the economy, business taxes in 2005 reached the second lowest level since the Depression.

Molly Ivins and Lou Dubose explain further the politics of how corporations have received such favorable treatment in the following bold pronouncement:

> Public policy is sold to the highest bidder. Less than one tenth of 1 percent of Americans gave 83 percent of all campaign contributions in the 2002 elections.

The big donors are getting back billions in tax breaks, subsidies, and the right to exploit public land at ridiculously low prices. The corporations that paid zero taxes from 1996 to 1998 include AT&T, Bristol-Myers, Squibb, Chase Manhattan, Enron, General Electric, Microsoft, Pfizer, and Philip Morris. Those same companies gave $150.1 million to campaigns from 1991 to 1998 alone and perennial legislation to gut the alternative minimum tax. [8]

In addition, corporations escape, evade, and avoid paying taxes through a number of means: by establishing offshore accounts; by devising arcane tax shelters and transfers of funds that the understaffed IRS cannot track; and sometimes by simply cheating. In fact, corporations are paying 30 percent less of their profits to the IRS than they did 20 years ago. The Reagan–Bush–Clinton–Bush, Jr. "revolution" has been, in effect, a reverse Robin Hood era—take from the poor and middle class and give to the rich. Harvard economist Mihir Desai estimates that "Corporations have managed to avoid as much as $54 billion in taxes by hiding about $155 billion in profits in tax shelters." [9] As corporations and wealthy individuals pay less and less, the burden of providing revenue for the federal government falls increasingly upon the backs of average workers, and services for our children and poor people are cut and cut. As Gore Vidal writes of George W. Bush's massive tax cuts for the rich, "Thus he made it clear that he too [like his father] favors socialism for the rich and free enterprise for the poor." [10]

Citizens for Tax Justice, a nonprofit research organization, reported that "a startling surge in corporate tax welfare is expected to drive corporate income taxes over the next two years down to only 1.3 percent of the gross domestic product. That will be the lowest level since the early 1980s—and the second lowest level in at least six decades." [11]

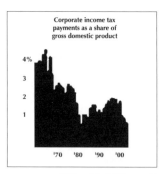

Corporate income tax payments as a share of gross domestic product

(*New York Times,* Oct. 8, 2004)

In short, this surge in corporate tax welfare has "allowed many companies to earn billions in profits, yet pay little or nothing in federal income taxes." [12]

Cheating

As mentioned earlier, it isn't just that corporations receive taxpayer-funded subsidies: corporations also profit by good old-fashioned cheating. One method of fattening the corporate coffers is by overstating assets. As David Cay Johnson writes:

> Investors, entrepreneurs and landlords annually avoid paying at least $29 billion in taxes by overstating the price of stocks, businesses and real estate, two professionals say in an article being published today in *Tax Notes*, an influential tax policy journal.
>
> Claiming to have paid more than the actual price for a stock, business, apartment building or piece of art results in a smaller profit being reported when the asset is sold, and a lower tax on that profit.
>
> An unpublicized problem of crisis proportions is plaguing the tax system, one that will cost the government at least $250 billion in the coming decade, the professors wrote. [13]

In addition to understating their profits, corporations have, Robert McIntyre asserts, "become increasing adept at shifting profits on paper from the states in which they *actually* earned into states that don't tax them." [14] Corporations have also adopted the technique of "almost permanently deferring their taxes by keeping money outside the United States in low-tax countries like Ireland or India." Edmund L. Andrews notes that "by maintaining deferral indefinitely, a taxpayer can achieve a result that is economically equivalent to 100 percent exemption of income." [15] Is this cheating? Technically, no, but the goal is clearly tax evasion and our social services and education are the losers.

Of course, the argument we hear all the time is that if we tax corporations more, jobs will flee overseas, companies will no longer be profitable, and so on. Nonsense. If corporations simply paid reasonable taxes, there would be ample profits, perhaps even higher dividends available to shareholders, and adequate remaining funds for research and development.

Providing our children with decent, effective schools ought to be our highest priority as a nation. In fact, even corporate executives give lip service to this notion. Why not actually *pay* the appropriate price and have everyone—even corporative executives—pay their fair share of the bill? We can have not only adequate but superb schools if we simply apply the principle of fairness and justice to corporate taxation.

NOTES:

1 Thom Hartman, *Unequal Protection* (New York: St. Martin's Press, 2002), p. 179.

2 Ibid., p. 181.

3 Warren Vieth, "Firms Often Avoided Taxes, *Los Angeles Times,* April 7, 2004, p. C.1.

4 Robert S. McIntyre, "They Make it Up. You Decide." *The American Prospect,* April 2005, p. 16.

5 Robert S. McIntyre, "It's Your Money They're Wasting." *The American Prospect*, November 2004, p. 16.

6 Charles Lewis and Bill Allison, *The Cheating of America: How Tax Avoidance and Evasion by the Super Rich Are Costing the Country Billions—and What You Can Do About It* (New York: Harper Perennial, 2002), p. 72.

7 Ibid.

8 Molly Ivins and Lou Dubose, *Bushwhacked: Life in George W. Bush's America* (New York: Vintage Books, 2003), p. 283.

9 Roy Ulrich, "And the Poor Pay Taxes, *The Nation,* June 2, 2003, p. 24.

10 Gore Vidal, *Imperial America: Reflections on the United States of Amnesia* (New York: Nation Books, 2004), p. 15.

11 Citizens for Tax Justice, "Institute on Taxation and Economic Policy, Tax Model," April 18, 2002.

12 Ibid.

13 David Cay Johnston, "Overstating Assets is Seen to Cost U.S. Billions in Taxes," *New York Times*, January 24, 2005, p. C2.

14 Robert S. McIntyre, "State Corporate-Tax Follies," *The American Prospect,* February 2005, p.17.

15 Edmund L. Andrews, "Congressional Study Notes Ways to Collect Billions More in Taxes," *New York Times*, January 28, 2005, p. A15.

CHAPTER 9

Cut Corporate Welfare

*No matter how cynical one becomes
it is never enough.*
—Lily Tomlin

We have heard over the past decades about the shameful and wasteful effects of welfare. Ironically, under a Democratic administration in the 1990s, we saw the demise of "welfare as we know it." The poor, struggling and often infirm individuals and families had their safety nets removed while everyone else felt virtuous and steadfast in requiring the deprived members of society to toughen up.

Meanwhile, another *un*necessary form of welfare—corporate welfare—went on unscathed, even enhanced. While some of the well-to-do in 2003 decried the handouts of some $193 billion to the poor (i.e., food stamps, aid to families with dependent children, nutrition to poor infants and children, Head Start) as "wastes" of public dollars, the government provided more than four times that amount—$815 billion—to corporations and wealthy individuals. [1]

Mark Zepenauer summarizes the truly astonishing scope of this welfare to the rich in the following catalog of handouts primarily to corporations:

Government Subsidies, Waste, Foregone Income	
Item	Cost ($ billions)
Social Security inequities	85
Tax breaks for homeowners	32.1
Runaway pensions	7.6
Tax avoidance by transnational corporations	137.2
Lower taxes on capital gains	89.8
Accelerated depreciation	85
Insurance loopholes	23.5
Business meals and entertainment	8.8
Tax-free municipal bonds	6.4
Export subsidies	1.8
Military waste and fraud	224
The S&L bailout	32
Agribusiness subsidies	30.5
Media handouts	14.2
Nuclear subsidies	10
Aviation subsidies	5
Mining subsidies	4.7
Oil and gas tax breaks	1.7
Timber subsidies	97.6
Tax credits for synthetic fuel development	60
Ozone tax exemptions	32
A bouquet of miscellaneous rip-offs	16.4

As Arianna Huffington writes in her 2003 book *Pigs at the Trough*, "There is no greater wrong—or hypocrisy—than the hard line taken against welfare for the working poor by the same people who don't bat an eyelid at the hundreds of billions of dollars doled out in corporate welfare." [2]

The reason why is clear: corporations fund political campaigns (70 percent to 80 percent of both parties) and elected (or "purchased") legislators pass legislation favorable to their "employers." Therefore, as welfare to the poor has been cut, welfare to the rich in the form of tax breaks and direct subsidies increases. The net result is that public services are depressed while profiteering soars.

There are other hidden subsidies that we simply overlook or that corporations have arrogated as their unquestionable rights when they are nothing of the sort. For example, Ralph Nader writes, "There is no serious public policy argument for why television broadcasters should be given control of the digital television spectrum—a $70 billion asset—for free." [3]

There is another category of subsidies that really requires a chapter— actually the subject requires a book to focus national attention—on subsidies leading to harmful consumption of environmental resources (see Chapter 17 of this book). Government subsidizes certain industries whose activities and policies are destructive to the planet's delicate membranes. As Michael Renner points out in the Worldwatch Institute's *State of the World 2004,* "Numerous subsidies allow the prices of fuels, timber, metals and minerals (and products incorporating these commodities) to be far lower than they otherwise would be, encouraging greater consumption." [4] A report by the Organization for Economic Cooperation and Development (OECD) estimates that global subsidies amount to about $1 trillion a year. Another study by Norman Myers and Jennifer Kent "puts perverse subsidies in six sectors—agriculture, energy, road transportation, water, fisheries, and forestry—at about $850 billion or more annually. In addition, there are about $1.1 trillion worth of quantifiable environment externalities [which] represent uncompensated costs that have to be borne by society at large and that, like subsidies, have distorting and detrimental impacts." [5] So the auto industry receives a subsidy, makes profits and evades taxes while its products—automobiles—foul the air, and citizen taxes pay to deal with air quality. A good deal for the industry, not such a good deal for everyone else. [6]

If we were to reduce and eventually eliminate these costly subsidies, we would accomplish several things:

1. Have more government funds available for badly needed social services and education;
2. Reduce the depletion of natural resources;
3. Have funds available for renewable energy, conservation, efficiency technologies, and the like.

It is, as Edward Galeano writes, an upside-down world we have created: We bankroll the already wealthy; through subsidies we encourage the depletion of the earth's resources; and we provide major subsidies for industries that produce weapons and systems of war. [7]

At the same time that financial aid is being handed out to corporations along with massive tax cuts, we as a society are unable to fund our schools properly. In reality there are billions of dollars available to our schools if our citizens and legislators simply discard the mind-set that somehow corporations are persons (a legal absurdity) whose rights transcend those of all American citizens and of our children.

Perhaps the most massive form of corporate welfare is to be found in the iron triangle of government-military-industry.

"Honesty is the best policy, Fernbaugh, but it's not company policy."

NOTES:

1 Mark Zepenauer and Arthur Naiman, *Take the Rich Off Welfare*, (Cambridge, MA: South End Press, 2004), p.3.

2 Arianna Huffington, *Pigs at the Trough* (New York: Crown Publishers, 2003), p. 147.

3 Ralph Nader, *Cutting Corporate Welfare* (New York: Seven Stories Press, 2000), pp. 14–15.

4 Michael Renner, *"Moving Toward a Less Consumptive Society,"* *State of the World 2004*, Worldwatch Institute (New York: W. W. Norton & Co., 2004), p. 98.

5 Ibid.

6 Tom Athanasious, *Divided Planet.* (Boston: Little Brown & Co., 1996), p. 264.

7 Edward Galeano, *Upside Down*, tr. Mark Fried, 2000 (New York: Henry Holt, 1990).

CHAPTER **10**

Billions for Defense Industries, Pennies for Schools

They shall beat their swords into plowshares,
and their spears into pruning-hooks; nation
shall not lift up sword against nation,
neither shall they learn war any more.
—Isaiah, II: 4

Every gun that is made, every warship launched,
Every rocket fired, signifies in the final sense a
Theft from those who hunger and are not fed, those
Who are cold and are not clothed.
—President Dwight D. Eisenhower,
April 16, 1953

The biggest subsidy of all is perhaps the one that is now questioned least—
the defense industry. President Eisenhower warned in 1958 against the
encroachment of political influence exercised by "the military–industrial
complex." Of course, the third partner in this complex, which is sometimes referred to as the "iron triangle," is the federal government itself, a
government now dominated by military–corporate transplants.

John Kenneth Galbraith comments in his book *The Economics of
Innocent Fraud,* "At this writing, corporate managers are in close alliance
with the President, the Vice President and the Secretary of Defense. Major corporate figures are also in senior positions elsewhere in the federal
government; one came from the bankrupt and thieving Enron to preside
over the Army." [1]

Disguised in the triangle is the private sector as public servant. The
corporations set the agenda for *military* spending and the *government* ap-
propriates funds or, to be more accurate, provides subsidies, and all three
are happy. The profits are immense, the power is almost total, and elected
officials get re-election funds, predominantly from corporations.

William Greider's sadly overlooked 1998 book *Fortress America* gives yet another illustration of why we do *not* have enough funds for desperately needed social and medical services, infrastructure renovations, or education. The nation has the money and the resources, but we squander them. Among Greider's findings are the following:

- We have so many tanks that the Army has taken to dumping them in the ocean to form coral reefs—and then asking to buy even more.
- The Air Force has so many long-range bombers it can't even afford to keep them in the air—and still it wants to build more.
- Strategic planning and training of our forces still focuses on fighting a Soviet-style superpower—even though none exists.
- Our tax dollars subsidize the R&D for weapons systems—and then arms dealers turn around to sell those systems to other countries.
- Budget constraints compel the armed forces to choose between soldiers and weapons—and they choose weapons, closing bases, discharging soldiers and weakening our troop strength.
- Fifteen years ago there were over twenty major arms manufacturers and lots of competition—now there are three, and the prices those companies charge have escalated beyond all reason. [2]

What is most disturbing about the government promotion of arms sales that benefit private corporations is not just the profiteering at the expense of the taxpayers, but the uses to which these arms are put. For example, in 2004 Lockheed Martin Corporation sold F-16 warplanes to Israel, which spent much of its $1.8 billion aid from the U.S.A. to buy them. Thus U.S. taxpayers fatten Lockheed's profits and no one blinks an eye. Our government claims it lacks the funds to help our schools, yet it has the funds to promote the sales of weapons. Particularly distressing is the fact that these weapons financed by and distributed by the U.S. have later been used against *our own soldiers* in Haiti, Panama, Somalia, Afghanistan, and Iraq.

The United States spends billions in a myriad of programs and agencies to support corporate commercial arms exports, according to the World Policy Institute's William Hartung. The Pentagon maintains a large bureaucracy devoted to promoting sales of military hardware by U.S. corporations to foreign governments. "The Defense Department spends millions at military air shows to hawk the arms makers' wares, and it spends billions of dollars on loans, grants, credits, and cash payments to enable foreign governments to buy U.S. weapons." [3]

After the end of the Cold War, there were optimistic projections of how we, as a nation, could rebuild, reform, and revitalize ourselves with the "peace dividend" we would soon receive. Now that our Soviet enemy, which supposedly posed an imminent danger for more than 45 years, was defanged and fragmented, surely we could reduce the bloated defense budget? Wrong. In fact, each year the military defense budget has grown and grown, while cities, schools, and hospitals still go begging for funds.

A handful of organized terrorists with box cutters took down the Twin Towers, yet the Pentagon demands more and more billion-dollar stealth bombers. The military budget requests for 2004 were $399.1 billion. As Eric Alterman and Mark Green write, "Judged merely by the size, capabilities, and sophistication of its military forces, the United States had, following the fall of the Soviet Union, moved beyond the category of superpower into an entirely new and perhaps unprecedented realm. Because it spends more on its military than all of the rest of NATO combined, the extent of American military superiority has become gargantuan. To take just one illustration, the U.S. Navy boasts nine super-carrier battle groups ringed by cruisers and guarded by nuclear submarines, with a tenth under construction. The world's closest competitor has zero. What about America's air force? The United States currently has more advanced fighters and bombers than all of the other nations of the world combined. It deploys three separate types of stealth aircraft (the B-1 and B-2 bombers and the F-16 fighter) with two more (the F-22 and F-35 fighters) about to go into production. Again, the world total for all America's competitors? None."[4] As Paul Krugman points out, "The military buildup seems to have nothing to do with the actual threat [of terrorism], unless you think that al Quaida's next move will be a frontal assault by several heavily armored divisions."[5]

If anyone doubts the half-literal and half-metaphoric title of this chapter (Billions for Defense Industries, Pennies for Education), then they might consider the following:

A. The Bush Administration in a year and a half spent nearly the same amount spent at the halfway point of the 15-year Vietnam War.

B. The Bush Administration's spending in Iraq, $4.7 billion a month, is almost the same—in 2004 dollars—as the Vietnam era spending of $5 billion per month.

C. The soon-to-be-spent $216 billion on Iraq is, as Derrick Z. Jackson writes: [6]

   ◆ Near four times the budget of the Education Department;
   ◆ Nearly double what the General Accounting Office said in the mid-1990s was needed to repair the nation's schools;
   ◆ 24 times what it would cost to fully fund the congressional appropriation for No Child Left Behind;
   ◆ 43 times what it would cost to enroll the 40 percent of eligible preschoolers still not in Head Start;
   ◆ 848 times the cost of the Even Start family literacy program, which Bush proposed to kill;
   ◆ 1,800 times the appropriation for the national math-science partnership between high schools and colleges, which Bush proposed to kill;
   ◆ 6,352 times the cost of a program to help pay secondary school counselors, which Bush proposed to kill;
   ◆ 12,000 times the cost of a national writing project, which Bush proposed to kill;
   ◆ 19,600 times the cost of a program to support "gifted and talented" students, which Bush proposed to kill;

D. On October 1, 2004, the *New York Times* reported that "amid one of greatest military spending increases in history, the Pentagon is starved for cash. The U.S. will spend more than $500 billion on national security in the year beginning today." [7]

This spending of greater than the combined defense spending of all the nations in the world is, as the *New York Times* continues, "a bonanza for the nation's armaments contractors." It is not, however, a bargain for health, education, and the general welfare.

How Has All This Come About?

How, we wonder, has all this come about? How has such a monumental disparity grown between U.S. military might and the rest of the world? Is it a runaway train? Is it paranoia of staggering proportions? Is it imperialism run amok? These are questions which a new flurry of books have raised and sought to answer. Once again, John Kenneth Galbraith has addressed these issues.

Galbraith begins his study with the premise: "Reality is more obscured by social or habitual preference and personal or group pecuniary advantage in economics and politics than in any other subject." [8] The key phrases here are "obscuring reality" and "pecuniary advantage."

The myth we live by today is that we have a market economy in which consumer demand drives what is produced. The public wants; the private sector delivers. Meanwhile, the general public is fed a steady diet of rhetoric praising a "free market economy," which, unfortunately, simply does not exist. The reality is "that the gross domestic product (GDP) is determined not by the public at large, but by the private suppliers. A large and expanding part of what is called the public sector is for all practical effect in the private sector." [9]

Now, to apply this to military subsidies and the increasing appetite of private military–industrial–defense corporations, let us look at the fiscal year 2003. Galbraith points out that "Close to *half* of the total of United States government discretionary expenditure. . .was used for military purposes—for defense, as more favorably it is currently called. A large part was for weapons procurement or for weapons innovation and development." [10] These expenditures are not the result of public debate. Though the Pentagon is referred to as the public sector, it is increasingly clear that corporations call the shots. Consider, for example, the United States' (and, for that matter,) the world's, largest military contractor, Lockheed Martin: nearly 80 percent of its revenue comes from the U.S. government and "most of the rest comes from foreign military sales, many financed with tax dollars." To paraphrase Ralph Waldo Emerson, corporations are in the saddle, and they ride humankind. Or as another writer, Danielle Brian puts it: "The fox isn't guarding the henhouse. He lives there." [11]

Chalmers Johnson adds a corollary, or perhaps a parallel, to Galbraith. Not only has the private sector taken over the American economy, Johnson adds that militarism is the driving force to America's economy, government, and role in the world. The dimensions of this militarism are as secret as they are immense. Johnson, perhaps more depressed and defeatist than others, believes the imperial-militarism is now pretty much a done deal and that its tentacles are so widespread and powerful as to be virtually unassailable and probably irreversible. Johnson points to a "vast empire of military bases that [has] sprung up more or less undetected and that is today a geopolitical fact of life." [12] He also refers to the 2001 Stockholm International Peace Research Institute (SIPRI) Yearbook which shows that "Global military spending rose to $798 billion in 2000, an increase of 3.1 percent from the previous year. The United States accounted for 37 percent of that amount, by far the largest proportion. It was also the world's largest arms salesman, responsible for 47 percent of all munitions transfers between 1996–2000." [13]

The Implications of Military Spending
By 2002, the United States' share of the total defense spending of all countries in the world was at 40 percent and rising. *The U.S.A. spends as much as the next nine countries combined.* [14] "In terms of sheer military dominance," writes Clyde Prestowitz in *Rogue Nation,* "The world has never seen anything like this." [15] Of course, what it means is fewer and fewer funds are available for human and societal relief. To illustrate the impact of the federal military budget: "only a 15% cut in the Pentagon budget—which military experts agree would not hurt our war-making powers one bit—could do all of these things:

- Rebuild America's public schools over the next 10 years: $12 billion;
- Feed and provide basic health care to all the world's poor: $12 billion;
- Reduce class size in grades 1 through 3 to 15 students per class: $11 billion;
- Reduce the debts of impoverished nations: $10 billion;
- Buy health coverage for every uninsured American child: $6 billion;
- Increase federal funding for clean energy and energy efficiency: $6 billion;
- Publicly finance all federal elections: $1 billion;
- Fully fund the Head Start program: $2 billion. [16]

Chalmers Johnson also exposes the staggering overall capacity of our nuclear arsenal and "the lack of any national connection between nuclear means and nuclear ends [as] further evidence of the rise to power of a military mindset." [17] What the public has failed to see is how this mindset interferes with funding adequacy in our schools, sustainability in our eco-systems, and decency and equity in our society. As Johnson states, "The habitual use of imperial methods over the space of forty years has become addictive." [18] It is high time to kick the habit.

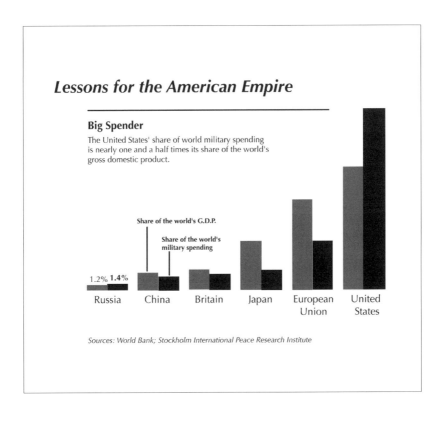

Lessons for the American Empire

Big Spender
The United States' share of world military spending is nearly one and a half times its share of the world's gross domestic product.

Share of the world's G.D.P.

Share of the world's military spending

1.2% **1.4%**

Russia   China   Britain   Japan   European Union   United States

Sources: World Bank; Stockholm International Peace Research Institute

NOTES:

1 John Kenneth Galbraith, *The Economics of Innocent Fraud: Truth for Our Time* (Boston: Houghton Mifflin Company, 2004), p.36.

2 William Greider, *Fortress America: The American Military and the Consequences of Peace* (New York: Public Affairs, 1998).

3 Ralph Nader, Cutting Corporate Welfare (New York: Seven Stories Press, 2000), p. 104.

4 Eric Alterman and Mark Green, *The Book on Bush: How George W. (Mis)Leads America* (New York: Penguin Group, 2004), p. 186.

5 Paul Krugman, *The Great Unraveling: Losing Our Way in the New Century* (New York: W. W. Norton and Company, 2003), p. 176.

6 Derrick Z. Jackson, "U.S. Education Suffers in Waste of Iraq War," *Liberal Opinion Week*, May 17, 2004, p. 26.

7 Tim Weiner, "A Vast Arms Buildup, Yet Not Enough for Wars," *The New York Times*, October 1, 2004, p. C1.

8 Galbraith, *Innocent Fraud*, p. ix.

9 Ibid., p. 34.

10 Ibid.

11 Danielle Brian, quoted in "Lockheed and the Future of Warfare," *The New York Times*, November 28, 2004.

12 Chalmers Johnson, *The Sorrows of Empire: Militarism, Secrecy and the End of the Republic* (New York: Metropolitan Books, 2004), p. 11.

13 Ibid., p. 63.

14 Andrew Bacevich, *The New American Militarism: How Americans Are Seduced by War* (Oxford and New York: Oxford University Press, 2005).

15 Clyde Prestowitz, *Rogue Nation: American Unilateralism and the Failure of Good Intentions* (New York: Basic Books, 2003), p. 26.

16 Jim Hightower, ed., "How Did We Get Into This Handbasket?" *The Hightower Lowdown*, February 2003.

17 Johnson, *Sorrows*, p. 64.

18 Ibid., p. 65.

> *I never intend to adjust myself to*
> *The madness of militarism.*
> —Martin Luther King, Jr.

Interlude

"Who was one of the biggest winners on November 21 2004? Some bloke named Jerry Jones. He ran a $5 million ad blitz in Arlington, Texas, to win a vote that will put $325 million of government money in his own pocket. Jerry's the billionaire owner of the Dallas Cowboys, and the vote was to get taxpayers to build a luxury sports palace for his private business.

He's just one of the billionaire sports owners across America who professes to love private enterprise but shamelessly wallow in corporate welfare. Local politicians, eager to please these moneyed power brokers, back their billionaire boondoggles even as basic needs in their cities go begging.

Take New York City, where both Mayor Michael Bloomberg and Governor George Pataki have rushed to the aid of Robert Wood Johnson IV, known to his pals and political cronies as Woody. Wood is heir to the Johnson & Johnson fortune, a backer of various far-right-wing causes, one of the top Republican donors in the country and owner of the New York Jets.

It's in this latter capacity that Woody, a fervent free enterpriser, wants a government handout. He says his team must have a new stadium to play in and both Bloomberg and Pataki are offering $600 million from New York taxpayers to build Wood a for-profit playground on a stretch of Manhattan's most valuable land.

These are the same two political leaders who keep shortchanging New York's school kids, claiming there's just no money to meet their needs. Most New York City schools have an asphalt playground no larger than Woody's garage, classrooms are dangerously dilapidated, parents and teachers have to chip in to buy most basic classroom supplies, and some school bathrooms don't have toilet paper!"

—*The Hightower Lowdown* (December 2004)

CHAPTER 11

Eliminate Offshore Tax Shelters

Put money in thy purse.
—Shakespeare,
Othello

This book is an attempt to delineate how we could at least provide all our children with an adequate, even a high-quality, education as a major step towards a level playing field. Requiring corporations to pay their fair share of taxes and preventing them from engaging in the massive tax evasions they now practice would provide enormous sums for education. In fact, a Congressional study issued on January 27, 2005 concludes that "The nation's system for taxing overseas profits of American corporations is so flawed that the government would save $55 billion if it simply scrapped the system altogether." [1] Fairness in taxation and prevention of devious and even illegal tax evasion seem not unreasonable demands. Both reforms *are* possible. The ridiculously low tax rates (for those who bother to comply) now allowed corporations are the result of legislation passed mostly in the last 22 years. Similarly the off-shore scams, tax avoidance and outright tax evasion result from laws passed by the legislative and executive beneficiaries of corporate campaign donations. It is a cozy club that excludes most Americans. In fact, the former head of the Internal Revenue Service, Republican Charles Rossotti, says that because of the IRS' diminished capacity, promoters and some tax professionals are selling a wide range of tax schemes and devices designed to improperly reduce taxes to taxpayers based on the simple premise that they can get away with it. [2]

In a recent study, *Promises Betrayed,* Bob Herbert, an op-ed columnist for the New York Times, lays out the "great lengths – literally to the ends of the earth – to escape paying its fair share of taxes to the government" that Halliburton has gone. [3] Note: the key phrase is "fair share." For example, in 2002 Halliburton paid just over $15 million to the

IRS. As Herbert comments, "That is effectively no money at all to an empire like Halliburton." [4] Halliburton's evasion is simply stealing money from our children's education.

How can we break out of this vicious circle? Education, education, education. The difficulty, of course, is that the poor don't vote, they don't contribute campaign dollars, and they can't offer perks to politicians. Hence, they are ignored and underserved. The existing laws serve the wealthy few, and the wealthy few see to it that those who are elected leave the laws alone—or distort them so that the wealthy can become even more wealthy.

The first step towards any possible reform is consciousness. And consciousness is a result of education. So we are back at the dilemma of how to free schoolchildren from the prison of poverty and neglect. How do we remove the foxes from their posts at the chicken coops?

The existing laws that allow offshore tax shelters are, to be sure, laws by and for their beneficiaries. To change these laws would almost certainly require campaign finance reform, where a Catch-22 applies. The people who benefit from existing ways of funding elections have already been elected by that system, and hence are unwilling to make changes. Thus, we have a tidy, though corrupt and undemocratic, system whereby wealthy individuals and corporations fund the elections of legislators who then pass and protect laws benefiting their benefactors. The only people hurt by this insider trading are the other citizens of America.

Consider, for the moment, tax evasion, known by the gentler term "tax shelters." It is estimated that corporate tax shelters robbed states of $12.4 billion in 2001. According to a 2003 study of the Multistate Tax Commission, a nonpartisan coalition of state taxing authorities, "Companies sheltering their assets overseas are draining an additional $70 billion from the federal treasury—funds that often make their way back to the states through programs such as Head Start or Americorps." [5] Thus a total of $82.4 billion in taxes was evaded in 2001.

The IRS's assessment is about the same. "The IRS estimates that U.S. corporations and rich individuals cost the country about $75 billion a year by setting up phony headquarters or residences in offshore havens like Bermuda and the Cayman Islands . . . Among the corporate tax haven users have been Harken Energy, which set up an offshore tax dodge while G. W. Bush was on its board, and Halliburton, which under Vice President Cheney's leadership went from nine to at least 44 offshore tax dodges." [6] So shall we expect the current administration to exercise leadership in eliminating these dodges and recovering the funds for projects needed to benefit society?

What is the extent of offshore tax sheltering, and how do the shelters function? According to Charles Lewis and Bill Allison in *The Cheating of America* (2001), "Today there are more than three million corporations operating worldwide with no identifiable owner. Virtually untaxable, offshore bank deposits. . .are now estimated at $3 trillion and rising. The offshore destination of choice is the Cayman Islands, with 585 banks and $700 billion in deposits." [7] The extent of the evasion is massive; in fact, most experts believe it is far greater than their worst estimates simply because it is all so convoluted, and because the IRS simply lacks the personnel to track the malfeasance down. As Paul Krugman writes, "We're losing revenue because profitable U.S. companies are using fancy footwork to avoid paying taxes." [8] Again, the rich can afford to find ways for not paying their taxes; the unemployed and the poor pay theirs.

The extent of this secrecy can be made clear by a few more facts:

1. There are some 55 offshore zones.
2. Secrecy havens have 1.2 percent of the world's population, and 26 percent of the world's wealth, including 31 percent of the net profits of U.S. multinationals.
3. In 2000, one-third of the wealth of the world's richest individuals, nearly $6 trillion of $17.5 trillion, was held offshore.
4. Today, offshore is where most drug money is laundered, estimated at up to $500 billion a year, more than the total income of the world's poorest 20 percent. "Add the proceeds of tax evasion and the figure skyrockets to $1 trillion." [9]

The impact of all this tax avoidance is staggering. In fact, the IRS estimates that taxpayers fail to pay more than $100 billion in taxes annually due on income from legal sources. The General Accounting Office says that American wage earners report 97 percent of their wages, while self-employed persons report just 11 percent of theirs. Each year between 1989 and 1995, a majority of corporations, both foreign- and U.S.-controlled, *paid no U.S. income tax.*

How does this "fancy footwork" work? Basically, a U.S. firm can incorporate, say, in Bermuda just by opening an office and thereby can shelter its overseas U.S. profits from taxation. Or, as Paul Krugman remarks, "Better yet, the company can then establish 'legal residence' in a low tax jurisdiction like Barbados, and arrange things so that its U.S. operations are mysteriously *un*profitable, while the mail drop in Barbados earns money hand over fist. In other words, this isn't about competition, it's about tax evasion." [10] It's also about cheating Americans out of funds badly needed for education, health and welfare. As hotel owner and tax cheat Leona Helmsley said before going off to jail, "Only poor people pay taxes."

For politicians to tell the public that we must cut social welfare and educational programs, endure having 45 million Americans without medical care, and permit homelessness without eliminating the corporate robbing of the federal coffers as outlined above is scandalous. We have the funds to take care of people who need and deserve care. If we truly believe in moral values, all we need to do is to require "the haves" to pay their fair share.

NOTES:

1 Edmund L. Andrews, "Congressional Study Notes Ways to Collect Billions More in Taxes," *New York Times*, Jan. 28, 2005, p. A 15.

2 Charles Rossotti as quoted in Samuel Loewenberg, "Offshore Thing," *The American Prospect,* March 2004, pp. 30–33.

3 Bob Herbert, *Promises Betrayed: Waking Up From the American Dream.* New York: Henry Holt & Co., 2005, pp. 260–61.

4 Ibid.

5 Arianna Huffington, "Corporate Tax Cheats Wreak Havoc on the Needy," *Los Angeles Times*, July 23, 2003, editorial page.

6 Robert L. Borosage, "Sacrifice is for Suckers," *The Nation*, April 28, 2003, pp. 4–5.

7 Charles Lewis and Bill Allison, *The Cheating of America* (New York: Harper Collins Books, 2002), pp. 265–266.

8 Paul Krugman, *The Great Unraveling: Losing Our Way in the New Century.* (New York: W. W. Norton and Company, 2003), p. 181.

9 Lucy Komisar, "Offshore Banking: The Secret Threat to America," *Dissent*, Spring 2003, pp. 45–51.

10 Krugman, *The Great Unraveling*, p. 181.

CHAPTER 12

Require Transnational Corporations to Pay Appropriate Taxes

To raise the standard of living of any man [and woman]
in the world is to raise the standard by some slight degree
for every man [and woman] everywhere in the world.
—Wendell L. Willkie,
One World

If our country's elected government officials truly dedicated themselves to improving the lives of all our citizens, they would attack tax evasion wherever it exists, since taxes lost are funds denied to health, education, and social improvement programs.

One major category of tax evaders is described by Susan Strange as "Transnational firms intent on avoiding tax and the number of tax havens helping them to do so." [1] As Galbraith points out in *The Economics of Innocent Fraud*, the lines between the public and private sector at this level seem hopelessly blurred. [2] Strange characterizes this phenomenon as parallel authority: "They [Trans National Corporations] are increasingly exercising a parallel authority alongside governments in matters of economic management" and "have encroached on their [governments'] domains of power." [3] Little wonder that they exercise this power *not* to pay taxes.

Kevin Danaher notes that "More than a quarter of the world's economic activity now comes from the 200 largest corporations. . .this means that prices are set, not by the mystical forces of the free market, but by corporate administrators who can arrange to have profits show up in tax havens and accomplish other miracles of creative accounting that improve the global bottom line." [4]

The loss of income from multinational companies avoiding taxes is immense. A recent study appearing in *Tax Notes* (the research done by a former Treasury Department economist) shows that American multinational companies booked a record $149 billion of profits in tax-haven countries in 2002. [5]

What then do the TNCs do with their power? History notes that:

1. They design and have enacted by their governmental partners a series of corporate deductions (the oil companies are a blatant example).
2. They award themselves—management and CEOs—enormous benefits and perquisites.
3. They participate directly in the shifting of the tax burden onto individual citizens and small businesses.

In addition, they make substantial contributions to the elected officials of their various governments.

What could be done about this situation? David Korten suggests one positive step: a 0.5 percent "Tobin Tax" on international financial transactions. This 0.5 percent tax, proposed more than fifteen years ago by Yale economist and 1981 Nobel Prize winner James Tobin, would impose "a small tax on the purchase and sale of financial instruments such as stocks, bonds, foreign currencies, and derivatives that would discourage very short-time speculation and arbitraging and remove an important source of unearned financial profit." [6] Such a tax would, according to William K. Tabb, [7] raise about $45 billion a month and could apply to debt reduction of poor countries and operations of the United Nations. Also, the U.S.A. could allot a portion to education in impoverished neighborhoods.

A second step would be the creation of an international tax code to prevent corporations' massive escape from taxes "by gaming the tax codes of various nations." As William Greider writes, "The dispersal of production opened the door to complicated accounting strategies in which companies shifted corporate tax liabilities from high-tax to low-tax nations, taking the business deductions where tax rates were high and claiming the income where rates were low. No one has succeeded, so far as I could discover, in estimating the total revenue losses to governments around the world, but it amounted to scores of billions of dollars, probably hundreds of billions." [8] An international tax code would return these billions of dollars to the people of the various countries where starvation, educational deprivation, health crises, and homelessness are legion—including the United States.

It would be difficult to calculate the billions of dollars lost to society each year in this one arena alone. Head Start centers, after-school programs, daycare and pre-school programs, arts in and after school, community arts centers, and recreation centers—all struggle, face cutbacks and outright elimination while transnational CEOs reward themselves with tax-free incomes, stock options, first-class travel to golf courses all over the world, massive "golden handshake" severance payments and the like. Little children are denied pre-school programs while the children of the TNC/CEOs receive every blessing known to man.

As the old saying goes, "The poor have always been with us," and so too have greed and caste-based systems, but it is also true that this situation need not be so. I do not expect beneficiaries of injustice to be the ones to reform injustices, but it would be a refreshing change if a simple sense of fairness and just a minimal redistribution of wealth and opportunity were to emerge somewhere in our national consciousness.

This sense of justice will, however, probably have to be forced upon leaders. It will need to come from the grassroots. Billions of dollars are being denied children and people in need in America and all over the globe. Fair play needs to be set in motion.

NOTES:

1 Susan Strange, *The Retreat of the State: The Diffusion of Power in the World Economy* (Cambridge, UK: Cambridge University Press, 1996), p. 62.

2 John Kenneth Galbraith, *The Economics of Innocent Fraud* (Boston: Houghton Mifflin, 2004), pp. 33–37.

3 Strange, *Retreat*, p. 65.

4 Kevin Danaher, *Corporations Are Gonna Get Your Mama* (Monroe: Common Courage Press, 1996), p. 36.

5 Martin Sullivan, "U.S. Multinationals Profit From Tax Havens," *Tax Notes*, September 27, 2004.

6 David C. Korten, *When Corporations Rule the World* (West Hartford: Kumarian Press, 1995), p. 313.

7 William K. Tabb, *The Amoral Elephant: Globalization and the Struggle for Social Justice in the Twenty-first Century* (New York: Monthly Review Press, 2001), p. 207.

8 William Greider, *One World, Ready or Not* (New York: Touchstone, 1998), p. 95.

Part III

Correcting Existing Systems:
Individuals

*You can have wealth concentrated in the hands
of a few, or democracy. You cannot have both.*
— Supreme Court Justice Louis Brandeis

Preface

It might be a useful exercise to pause and remind ourselves why we, good readers, are struggling to learn how we might discover and recover the funds necessary to achieve quality education for our children and youth.

We saw in the previous section (II) that U.S. multi-national corporations avoid and sometimes illegally cheat governments out of billions of dollars of revenue. Meanwhile, around the globe, inner city and impoverished rural areas provide children with sub-standard or no education at all. Wherever this is true, the powers that be cry poor and claim they lack the funds to rectify these conditions.

We *do* have the resources to act when those with power reward themselves and deny others. Restoring corporate taxes to a reasonable level, cutting corporate welfare, reducing defense spending, eliminating off-shore shelters, and applying tax codes to transnational corporations would yield enough funds to provide every child on earth with a decent education. This is just the start of what we *could* do if we had the will, if we shifted our priorities, and if we demanded and received leadership.

Now let's look at some ways to restore fair play in the arena of individual taxation.

CHAPTER 13

Estate Taxes: Myths and Realities

Oh the rich get richer and the poor get poorer,
in the mornin', in the evenin', ain't we got fun?
—Popular song

MYTH 1:

We can receive/enjoy critical public services without paying for them.

Somehow, those who control the creation and manipulation of public opinion have pulled off a self-serving coup: they have convinced the public that taxes are evil and that pre-tax income should be the exclusive possession of each citizen. This conveniently ignores the fact that taxes provide governmental services for "the general welfare," as mandated by the Constitution and as enjoyed by all of us—rich and poor. Our highways, bridges and roads, postal services, health care (where it exists), water, police, National Guard, armed forces—all these government services provide the conditions under which we can conduct business and live our lives peacefully and productively.

MYTH 2:

Estate taxes harm "the little guy/common man."

Myth number two is that the form of taxes known as estate taxes will harm the common man, the small farmer, the general populace. The myth was promoted by candidate George W. Bush, Jr. in Iowa in 2000 when he proclaimed, "To keep farms in the family, we are going to get rid of the death tax." He was referring to the estate tax. The truth: "True stories of farmers losing the farm to the estate tax are so rare that numerous experts and investigators were unable to find *any* real examples." [2] In fact, "Only one in eight of the 49,863 taxable estates in 1999 had *any* farm assets and the average value was well under the threshold to trigger estate taxes." [2] Ironically, eliminating the estate tax is actually a threat to small farmers, in that it enables greater accumulation of wealth to be concentrated in fewer big farmers' hands.

96

The myth of "the death-tax-as-killer-of small businesses" has also been effectively promoted to apply beyond small farms. Again, the reality is that there is virtually no evidence that this is so. None. The purpose of estate taxes is to provide opportunities for those who are playing on an *un*level field. In reality, estate taxes are borne by a small percentage of immensely wealthy people who, after having paid their estate taxes, are still immensely wealthy. The income would have a much more powerful impact on the "general welfare" of society.

Who really pays those taxes? "The estate tax is a transfer tax imposed on large accumulations of wealth when someone dies. Its exemptions are so high that it falls on the heirs of fewer than two percent of estates every year." [3] In fact, in 2004, fewer than one percent of people who died paid any estate tax at all. [4] As David Cay Johnston writes in *Perfectly Legal,* "America doesn't tax death. It's an estate tax, and it only kicks in for a married couple at $3 million." [5] Furthermore, these exemptions will more than double by 2009. Thus we see that trying to frighten small farmers and small businesses and 98 percent of our citizens about so-called "death taxes" is cynical, irresponsible, and simply wrong.

The potential income is, however, significant and could help improve our schools, health care systems, inner-city conditions, and the like. To give but one startling example of possible uses: in 2003 the World Health Organization estimated that $10 billion spent on antibiotics and insecticide-treated mosquito nets would save 8 million lives a year—many of them children. Consequently, estate tax with an exemption of $5 million (which in 1999 would apply to only 3,300 estates with an average of $16 million each) would leave each estate with $11 million of its $16 million, and would have generated $20 billion in revenues. Half of that would have saved the lives of 8 million people. [6]

Perhaps the most disturbing aspect of the Bush plan for the reduction of and the phasing out of the estate tax is the creation of economic dynasties in America. Even billionaire Warren Buffett finds this an appalling prospect: "Without the estate tax, you will, in effect, have an aristocracy of wealth, which means that you pass down the ability to command the resources of the nation based on heredity rather than merit." [7] In fact, on the 1997 Forbes list of the 400 wealthiest Americans, "42 percent inherited enough wealth to be on the list without doing anything else." [8]

MYTH 3:

Estate Taxes Represent Unfair Double Taxation

Frequently we are told – by proponents of repealing the estate tax – that estate taxes represent an unfair brand of double taxation. This argument does not hold up to scrutiny. It's a nice phrase, easily remembered — "double taxation" – but it is a smoke screen. First of all, as we have seen, it only kicks in at levels that exempt 98% of Americans from being taxed at all. And secondly, "much of the wealth transferred at death has never been taxed. That's because capital gains on assets like homes, stocks and bonds are not taxed until the asset is sold. Obviously, if you inherit, say, a house, its owner didn't sell it, so never paid any capital gains tax on it." [9]

Again, we confront the fundamental issue: priorities. Do we believe that our highest priority is to allow a wealthy few to accumulate unlimited amounts of wealth or that we should provide a fair, decent, and sustainable society for all?

William H. Gates, Sr. and Chuck Collins phrase the question even more bluntly, "How high a price is America willing to pay in order to give a handful of millionaires and billionaires a tax break?" The question should answer itself.

NOTES:

1 William Gates and Chuck Collins, *Wealth and Our Commonwealth* (Boston: Beacon Press, 2002), pp. 66–67.

2 David Cay Johnston, *Perfectly Legal: The Covert Campaign to Rig Our Tax System to Benefit the Super Rich—and Cheat Everybody Else* (New York: Portfolio, 2003), p. 74.

3 Gates and Collins, p. 2.

4 *The Hightower Lowdown,* June 2005, p. 3.

5 Johnston, p. 73.

6 Paul Krugman, "Heart of Cheapness," *International Herald Tribune,* June 1–2, 2002, p. 4.

7 Warren Buffett, quoted in David Cay Johnston, "Dozens of Americans Join in Fight to Retain the Estate Tax," *New York Times*, February 14, 2001.

8 James Heintz and Nancy Folbre, *The Ultimate Field Guide to the U.S. Economy* (New York: The New Press, 2002), p. 20.

9 "Long Live Estate Tax," *New York Times*, April 15, 2005, p. A18.

CHAPTER 14

Tax Cuts: Priorities and Inequities

Washing one's hands of the conflict between the powerful
and the powerless means to side with the powerful,
not to be neutral.

—Paulo Freire

Leaving aside for the moment the motivation(s) behind the tax cuts of the last three Republican administrations—which have clearly favored the already rich—the net results to society at large are equally clear: "The government is broke, and most of the problem is due to the sharp decline in taxes paid by corporations and rich people." So writes Robert S. McIntyre, Director of Citizens for Tax Justice. [1] He continues with these staggering facts: The effective federal tax rate on the wealthiest one percent of Americans has dropped by 30 percent over the past quarter-century. To put that in perspective, if the wealthy paid the same share of their income in taxes today as they paid in 1977, annual tax revenues would jump by $200 billion. Likewise, if corporate income tax revenues were restored to their average share of the economy from 1950 to 2000, companies would pay $180 billion a year more. [2] This analysis, I might add, does not account for offshore tax shelters and outright cheating. So when we hear that we cannot afford adequate schools, we ought to shout out loud and clear, "Oh, yes, we can, if all citizens paid their fair share."

David Cay Johnston further illuminates this sorry state in his 2004 publication, *Perfectly Legal: The Covert Campaign to Rig Our Tax System to Benefit the Super Rich—and Cheat Everybody Else.* Johnson pulls few punches, and his statistics are ugly. For example, as the *Los Angeles Times* reports, "In 1993 the richest Americans paid 30 cents on the dollar in federal income taxes. . .at the end of the Clinton administration, they paid 22 cents on the dollar. And, when the Bush cuts came in, they go down further—to 17 ½ cents on the dollar. That means that the super-rich have gotten a 41 percent reduction in their tax burden." [3] In fact, David Cay Johnston points out that when *all* taxes are added in—state, local, federal income, etc.— "the top fifth of Americans pay just a penny more out of a dollar in taxes overall than the poorest fifth, 19 cents versus 18 cents." [4]

The gross inequities of this situation are gradually penetrating the public consciousness. For example, in April 2004, Allan Sloan noted that President Bush is showering "rewards on people who have already made it to the top rungs" and that ordinary taxpayers are providing more than their fair share of tax revenue to the government, while corporations and wealthy individuals are not. [5] Furthermore, David Cay Johnston observes, those Americans earning $10 million a year now pay a lesser share of their income in taxes than those making $100,000 to $200,000. [6]

It is difficult to avoid the conclusion that a group of conservative ideologues and plutocrats have consciously engineered a decline in the amount of government revenue available for social services. In fact, one conservative tax-cut promoter, Grover Norquist, is quite upfront about it all. He states that the goal "is to cut government in half in twenty-five years, to get it down to the size where we can drown it in the bathtub." An amusing comment until one realizes that down the bathtub drain with Mr. Bush's and Mr. Norquist's tax cuts go schools, hospitals, libraries, forests, waterways, city infrastructures, and the like. Arundhati Roy summarizes the consequences of the first three years of George W. Bush's administration: besides the loss of over a million jobs, exorbitant military expenses, massive corporate welfare, and huge tax cuts for the rich, according to a survey by the National Conference of State Legislatures, "U.S. states *cut* forty-nine billion dollars in public services, health, welfare benefits, and education in 2002." [7] As the U.S. population grows, how in the world can we shrink government-funded services? We can afford seemingly unlimited subsidies for big businesses and for the military–industrial clan, but we cannot afford decent schools, health care, and city services?

We Do Have the Money

In 2002, Charles Rossetti, chief of the Internal Revenue Service, tried to show that by increasing the number of IRS investigators, we could harvest billions of dollars from tax evaders. He argued that the IRS is "steadily losing the war with tax cheats, especially the wealthiest and most sophisticated among them." [8] According to national correspondent and author

Joe Conason, "An investment of $2 billion in law enforcement could net more than $70 billion in lost tax receipts annually." [9] This would seem a no-brainer to procure badly needed funds until we remember that the tax cheats contribute to politicians' campaign funds. So Rossetti's suggestions were not well received. They should have been, and the public should demand that the principle be applied. Since when is cheating acceptable?

In their new book *Bushwacked,* Molly Ivins and Lou Dubose are even more outspoken regarding the dismantling of the IRS to allow the wealthy to evade, avoid, and cheat the government:

> Under Newt Gingrich, Congress held grand-inquisitor hearings in which the IRS was denounced for "Gestapo tactics." The Republicans then passed a "tax reform" act that should have been called the Let's Hamstring the IRS So It Can't Make Rich People Pay Act. The result is that since 1995, the IRS has focused most of its tax-fraud investigations on the working poor. In April, 2003, the IRS announced it would be auditing more of the working poor.
>
> The decline in auditing rich people and corporations actually started fourteen years ago. In 2001, audits of the working poor increased by 48.6 percent. Those applying for the EITC have a one in 47 chance of being audited, while those making more than $100,000 have a one in 208 chance of getting audited. In 1988, that number for those over $100,000 was one in nine, according to the Institute for Public Affairs. [10]

Hidden In Plain Sight
An April 2004 report from the Corporation for Enterprise (www.cfed.org) further exposes the myth that we lack the funds to take care of our schools. Called "hidden in plain sight," the Ford Foundation-supported report totals up costs of the federal government's asset-building tax breaks and spending programs at $335 billion year—a stunning third of a trillion dollars." [11] CFED did further calculations to see how the tax cut largesse is distributed. It turns out that in the three largest areas of tax deductions, 34 percent of savings go to the top one percent of taxpayers (those whose incomes average over one million) and the bottom 60 percent receive less than five percent. As this book goes to press, new tax cuts are kicking in. On New Year's Day 2006, people who earn upward of $200,000 a year will be able to claim bigger write-offs for a spouse, their children, and other expenses,

like mortgage interest on a vacation home. Thus we see that the tax cuts of 2001, 2002, and 2003 are now joined with new tax cuts – for people who don't need the extra help. Yet, many of these same primary beneficiaries will sadly tell you that we just can't afford to fix our schools.

NOTES:

1 Robert S. McIntyre, "Loophole-Consolidation Program," *The American Prospect*, December 2003, p. 22.

2 Ibid.

3 Betti Jane Levine, "Beware the Ides of April," *Los Angeles Times*, April 7, 2004, pp. E1, E13.

4 Johnston quoted in Graydon Carter, *What We've Lost* (New York: Farrar, Straus and Giroux, 2004).

5 Allan Sloan, "Why Your Tax Cut Doesn't Add Up," *Newsweek,* April 12, 2004, pp. 41–47.

6 David Cay Johnston, "Richest Are Leaving Even the Rich Far Behind," *New York Times,* June 5, 2005. p.1.

7 Arundhati Roy, *An Ordinary Person's Guide to Empire* (Cambridge, MA: South End Press, 2004), p. 59.

8 Joe Conason, *Big Lies: The Right Wing Propaganda Machine and How It Distorts the Truth* (New York: Thomas Dunne Books, 2003), p. 28.

9 Ibid.

10 Molly Ivins and Lou Dubose, *Bushwhacked: Life in George W. Bush's America* (New York: Vintage Books, 2003), p. 42.

11 Ned Pierce, "Tax Largesse and Sharp Accounting: Predictable Winners—and Losers," *Liberal Opinion Weekly*, April 12, 2004, pp. 41–47.

> *All Taxes redistribute wealth: the question is, do we want that distribution to go up or down in the class structure?*
> —Kevin Danaher

Interlude

Fernando is a Mexican-American teacher at a public high school in Los Angeles. The school has over 4,000 students grades 9–12. Approximately 1800 are enrolled in the 9th grade and by the end of the 12th grade between 700–900 graduate.

Fernando has 6 classes a day of 40 students each class. He teaches an industrial arts class that requires extensive supplies. His budget is $1,000 a year. Consequently, he has supplemented his classes the past six years (1999–2004) with $60,000 ($10,000 a year) out of his own modest paycheck. He simply cannot teach his classes on $1,000 a year of supplies.

During this same time period Ken Lay received a five year total of at least $325 million in salary, bonuses, stock option gains and stock sales back to his company, Enron.

CHAPTER 15

CEO Pay: At the Trough

The salary of the chief executive of a large
corporation is not a market award for achievement.
It is frequently in the nature of a warm personal
gesture by the individual to himself. . .
                              —John Kenneth Galbraith

Another subject to consider when state and federal officials and legislators bemoan the lack of funds available for our nation's schools is CEO pay: again a question of priorities, values, and equity. Before proceeding, let us examine the chart below:

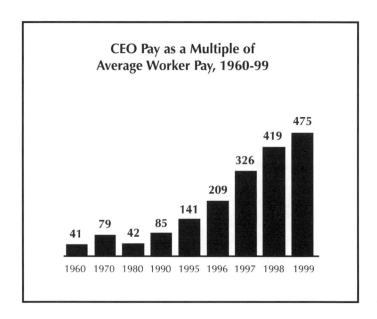

Source: *Business Week*, annual CEO Pay issues.

What this chart shows is the startling increases in CEO pay, both in absolute terms and relative to pay increases for workers. One does not have to be a card-carrying Marxist to be startled by the discrepancies: a simple sense of fairness and appropriateness will do.

Why is this a concern for our society, and how does it relate to improving our schools?

It is relevant because corporations and wealthy individuals not only amass great fortunes, but also use their wealth to influence legislation that then allows them to avoid paying taxes on that wealth. In the case of CEO pay, gargantuan salaries are self-awarded, allowed by passive, inattentive, or compliant boards of directors. Because of these salaries workers receive less pay or are laid off, and the economy is deprived of their potential spending and payroll taxes. In addition, dividends to stockholders are less than they might be. To cite but one blatant example of CEO pay: while the company's stock prices fell, in 2004 Viacom Inc. awarded its top three executives total compensation ranging from $52 million to $56 million! [1]

History shows us that when such large amounts of money are at stake, corruption, exploitation, and malfeasance rear their ugly heads. For some recent examples, consider:

1. Campaign contributions are tied to bigger contracts:

    ◆   Median CEO pay at the 37 largest defense contractors rose 79 percent from 2001 to 2002, while overall CEO pay combined rose only 6 percent.
    ◆   The size of campaign contributions by the largest defense contractors revealed a strong correlation between campaign contributions made by a company in the 2000 and 2002 elections and the value of defense contracts awarded to that company. [2]

2. Accounting scandals hurt workers, shareholders, and taxpayers:

    ◆   CEOs of companies under investigation for accounting irregularities earned 70 percent more from 1999 to 2001 than the average CEO at large companies.

◆ "Taxpayers shoulder the burden when corporations show different books to shareholders and the government." [3]

3. CEO salaries explode while worker pay stagnates:

◆ The average top executive in America receives over 400 times more in pay than the typical hourly employee in the same company. Compare this 400-to-1 ratio with those in countries competing with us in the global market, as reported recently by The Hightower Lowdown: [4]

Brazil	57 to 1
Mexico	45 to 1
Hong Kong	38 to 1
Britain	25 to 1
Australia	22 to 1
China	21 to 1
Italy	19 to 1
Spain	18 to 1
France	16 to 1

◆ The CEO–worker pay gap in 2000–2001 is between 411 and 475 to nearly 10 times that of 1982. Some say it is even as high as 531:1. [5]

◆ If the minimum wage had grown as fast as CEO pay since 1990, it would have been $21.41 an hour in 2001 instead of $5.15.

4. CEOs profit from layoffs, shortfalls, and tax dodges (See Chapter 11 on Offshore Tax Shelters):

- CEOs at companies with the largest layoffs, most under-funded pensions and biggest tax breaks were rewarded with bigger paychecks.
- Congress supported runaway CEO pay and helped U.S. companies avoid paying their fair share of taxes by blocking proposed stock option reforms ten years ago.

The stock option scheme is undoubtedly a crafty one. Many corporations boost their reported profits by not counting stock options as an expense in their financial statements to shareholders, then *deduct* these same stock options in their corporate tax returns. Thus, in 2002, "350 leading firms received an estimated $3.6 billion in tax deductions based on their CEOs filling their pockets with $9 billion in option gains." [6] As Arianna Huffington pointedly puts it, "More than just a way to pay off greedy CEOs, stock options have also proven to be a corporate accountant's wet dream—a versatile form of compensation that is not counted as an expense on company ledgers, and yet is fully deductible when it comes to chiseling the taxman." [7]

How have CEOs accumulated such power, one may wonder? Susan Strange, in her study, *The Retreat of the State,* offers one explanation. Since it was first observed in the 1930s by Adolf Berle, Gardiner Means, and James Burnham, there has been a "passing of power from shareholders to managers," [8] with the result that the managers have received, from accommodating and passive boards of directors, "a marked rise in rewards both in terms of salaries, of severance payments—golden handshakes or parachutes—and of stock options, to say nothing of the prerequisites of office in first-class air travel, expense accounts for restaurant bills and luxury hotel accommodation and not least the regiment of chauffeurs, gardeners, masseurs, social secretaries, even doctors, dentists and lawyers—who in olden times would have made up the retinue of landed aristocracy." [9]

To return to the issue of this book, what is the relationship of CEO pay to funding needy schools? Simply, an excess of funds spent in one area when there is a desperate need in another. For example, companies will often lay off workers, thus saving costs of both salaries and health benefits, then will turn around and award their CEOs even higher pay. In fact, since 1993 the average pay for CEOs of the S&P 500 companies has tripled to ten million, while the number of Americans without health insurance has increased by six million. Despite the public concern over corporate malfeasance, CEO pay continues to climb. In 2004, CEO pay increased by an average of 12.6 percent while the pay of average workers rose by 2.6 percent. [10]

A recent study by Lucian Bebchuk of Harvard and Yaniv Grinstein of Cornell showed that public companies devoted about 10 percent of their profits to compensating their top five executives, up from six percent in the mid-1990s. [11] It is, in effect, an absconding of corporate wealth by top managers. If corporations did not compensate their CEOs with such mammoth salaries, they would be able to pay more easily the taxes they now avoid, and they would be able to provide shareholders with even better returns.

Recently, New York's Attorney General Eliot Spitzer sued Dick Grasso (the former head of the New York Stock Exchange) under an obscure state law that regulates nonprofit institutions and requires that an executive be paid "reasonable compensation" that is "commensurate with the services performed." Reasonable people can debate what is reasonable compensation, but the recent bloated and growing CEO salaries—compared to workers'—seem *un*reasonable by any standards of decency, equity, and appropriateness. Once again, we see funds hoarded at the top and denied to the majority.

"We are prepared to offer you a compensation package that includes a significant portion of the Western Hemisphere."

NOTES:

1 Geraldine Fabrikant, "While Shares Fell, Viacom Paid Three $160 Million," *New York Times,* April 16, 2005, p. B1.

2 *United for a Fair Economy*, Boston, MA, September 4, 2003.

3 Ibid.

4 Jim Hightower & Phillip Frazer, "CEOs Pay Themselves $7,452 An Hour On Average," *The Hightower Lowdown,* June 2003 (Vol. 5, No. 6), pp. 1–4.

5 Geneva Overholser, "CEOs Get Richer," *Washington Post*, August 31, 2001.

6 *United for a Fair Economy*, Boston: September 4, 2003.

7 Arianna Huffington, *Pigs At the Trough* (New York: Crown Publishers, 2003), p. 45.

8 Susan Strange, *The Retreat of the State: The Diffusion of Power in the World Economy* (Cambridge, UK: Cambridge University Press, 1996), p. 64.

9 Ibid.

10 Associated Press, "Chief Executive Pay Increases 12.6% In '04," *Los Angeles Times,* April 25, 2005, p. C2.

11 Lucian Bebchuck & Yaniv Grinstein, "The Growth of Executive Pay," Discussion Paper No.510, April 2005. Harvard Law School, Cambridge, MA, p.1.

> *He who knows he has enough is rich.*
> —Lao-Tzu (3rd century B.C.)

Part IV

Creating New Sources
of Revenue

*We must show that greed and self-enrichment
for the few should not be – and really cannot
be – the way to a happy society for all.*
—Michael Parenti

Preface

In Part III we see how not only corporations but wealthy individuals have legislated themselves out of paying their fair share of societal support. We see that treating estate taxes with a modicum of reason, restoring tax cuts to the pre-Bush giveaways to the top 1%, and putting a lid on overblown CEO salaries could provide the funds to solve many of our educational and social problems. Furthermore, these three reforms would not jeopardize the social status or lifestyle of the very rich one iota; it would simply reduce the national disparities of wealth from obscene to gross. Now let's examine some other ways to move from inadequacy to excellence.

Once the oligarchy has been made stupid with insolence and greed, it's only a matter of time—maybe two or three decades, never more than three or four generations—before the government reformulates itself under a new row of statutes and a new set of glorious truths.
—Lewis Lapham,
Waiting for the Barbarians

CHAPTER 16

Wealth Taxes: Let's Be Fair

From everyone who has been given, much, much will be required.
—Luke: 12:48

The unavoidable fact is that the government has certain responsibilities. The discharge of those responsibilities costs monies.

—Paul Volcker,
Former Chairman,
The Federal Reserve

Fact: the rich are getting richer in America and the poor are getting poorer. Also, the economic gap between families of whites and families of color is widening. William H. Gates, Sr., certainly not a pauper nor a malcontent, and Chuck Collins ask an incisive question: "How high a price is America willing to pay in order to give a handful of millionaires and billionaires a tax break?" [1] Are we willing to see many schools and schoolchildren languish in squalor under disgraceful conditions? Is that the price?

Ray Boshara defines the current situation in these stark terms: "The United States is more unequal than at any other time since the dawn of the New Deal—indeed, it's the most unequal society in the advanced democratic world." [2] The statistics are shocking, yet somehow as a society we seem numbed and almost impervious to the extraordinary disparities in wealth and living conditions in America.

One thing is certain: the trends of the past 20 years threaten democracy itself and almost guarantee a permanent aristocracy as the growing disparities of wealth are passed from generation to generation. Level playing fields will soon be a quaint concept from the past as the majority of Americans are forever frozen in a class hierarchy.

Is this too drastic a scenario? Consider the following:

♦ In 1988 the top one percent of households owned 47 percent of the nation's total wealth; [3]

- From 1983 to 1998, The share of the top one percent of wealth holders rose by 5 percent;
- The wealth of the bottom 40 percent showed an absolute decline;" [4]
- From 1983 to 1998 the top 15 percent received almost 90 percent of the total increase in income and more than 90 percent of the increase in wealth. [5]

To further illustrate current conditions, David Cay Johnston writes, "In recent years the richest one percent of Americans, the top 1.3 million or so households, have owned almost half of the stocks, bonds, cash and other financial assets in the country. The richest 15 percent control nearly ALL of the financial assets." [6]

What is really happening beneath the radar screen is a shifting of the tax burdens from the already well-off to the struggling and poor families. According to David Cay Johnston, "When governments set tax rates, they are making decisions about who will prosper and by how much." [7] Many of the federal level decisions of the past 20 years seem to have had a clear agenda: to help the rich, to shift the burden to those of lesser means. On the surface it seems preposterous and totally unfair. In reality it is both. Johnston explains how this comes about, "Most Americans depend on wages for their income, wages that are tracked closely by government and leave little opportunity to escape taxes. The super rich are different. They largely control what the government knows about their incomes. [8] Is there anything to be done about this? Yes, there is. Edward N. Wolff, Professor of Economics at New York University, suggests we adopt what half of the 24 countries of the Organization for Economic Cooperation and Development (OECD) already do. We could impose direct taxation on household wealth. [9] The fundamental principle underlying a wealth tax is that of societal equity. The fundamental question leading to this principle is, What kind of a nation do we want to be? William Gates Sr. and Chuck Collins paint the stark picture that is emerging: "Our culture becomes more like an apartheid society, where haves and have nots no longer simply occupy opposite sides of the tracks, but inhabit wholly different worlds." [10]

One way to counter this avalanche away from democracy and towards aristocracy/oligarchy/ plutocracy is a wealth tax. This is not an inheritance tax or an estate tax, but a tax based on an annual reassessment of the total value of personal property. The concept of a wealth tax has been promoted forcefully by Wolff, who makes the following observations:

1. A wealth tax—even at modest levels for the wealthy—could generate at least $55 billion in revenue annually (a 2001 estimate).
2. Such a tax would cost even the wealthiest families less than the management fees for a typical mutual fund, while for three quarters of Americans it would cost practically nothing.
3. "An annual wealth tax may induce individuals to transfer assets from less productive uses to more productive ones." [11]
4. "There is no strong evidence that the presence of a wealth tax inhibits savings." [12]

Finally, the main reason for a wealth tax is to generate revenue to improve our schools and social conditions, to make a modest step towards providing equality of opportunity, and to counter the anti-democratic forces of class rigidity and inequity. It is a small price we would be asking the already rich to pay. Although it wouldn't even begin to reverse the disparities that have burgeoned in the past twenty years, it would be a welcome start.

NOTES:

1 William H. Gates, Sr., and Chuck Collins, "Tax the Wealthy," *The American Prospect*, June 17, 2002, pp. 20–21.

2 Ray Boshara, "The $6,000 Solution," *The Atlantic Monthly*, January/February 2003, pp. 91–95.

3 Edward N. Wolff, *Top Heavy: The Increasing Inequity of Worth in America and What Can Be Done About It* (New York: The New Press, 2002), p. 8.

4 Ibid., pp. 8–9.

5 Ibid., pp. 37–38.

6 David Cay Johnston, *Perfectly Legal: The Covert Campaign to Rig Our Tax System to Benefit the Super Rich—And Cheat Everybody Else* (New York: Portfolio, 2003), p. 11.

7 Ibid., p. 10.

8 Ibid., p. 13.

9 Wolff, p.67.

10 William H. Gates, Sr., and Chuck Collins, *Wealth and Our Commonwealth* (Boston: Beacon Press, 2002), p. 22.

11 Wolff, p. 69.

12 Ibid., p. 71.

Interlude

Between 1972 and 2001 the wage and salary income of Americans at the 90th percentile of the income distribution rose only 34 percent, or about 1 per cent per year. So being in the top 10 percent of the income distribution, like being a college graduate, wasn't a ticket to big income gains.

But income at the 99th percentile rose 87 percent; income at the 99.9th percent rose 181 percent; and income at the 99.99th percentile rose 497 percent. No, that's not a misprint.

Just to give you a sense of who we're talking about: the nonpartisan Tax Policy Center estimates that this year the 99th percentile will correspond to an income of $402,306, and the 99.9th percentile to an income of $1,672,726. The center doesn't give a number for the 99.99th percentile, but it's probably well over $6 million a year.

—Paul Krugman,
Graduates Versus Oligarchs
New York Times, 2-27-06

CHAPTER 17

Eco Taxes: Win, Win

Socialism collapsed because it did not allow the market to tell the economic truth. Capitalism may collapse because it does not allow the market to tell the ecological truth.
—Oystein Dahle,
Former Vice
President of Exxon for Norway

If we cannot imagine a healthy, bountiful, and sustaining environment today, it will delude us tomorrow.
—Mark Dowie

While much of the total U.S. tax burden has been shifted from corporations and wealthy individuals to ordinary taxpayers in the form of sales taxes (taxes on consumption, which are regressive), there is one consumption tax that is not only advisable, but critical: the so-called "Green Tax," or, as environmental research specialist Michael Renner urges in *Moving Toward a Less Consumptive Economy,* [1] an eco-tax on the consumption of environmentally threatened resources. Renner argues that the current tax systems "make natural resources use far too cheap and render labor too expensive. Eco-tax revenues would be used to lighten the tax burden now falling on labor, which would encourage job creation." [2]

Victor Vork, a fellow of the Worldwatch Institute, summarizes the basic principle of eco-taxes this way: "Tax lightly the things you want more of (labor and income) and tax more heavily what you want less of (resource depletion and pollution of the environment)." [3]

In addition, enlightening the public about the need for eco-taxes can help lead not only Americans, but all global citizens, to learn the need for *Alternate Economic Indicators.* The problem with our current belief that growth is our only available economic indicator is that it does not fit the needs of our world today. As Victor Anderson, researcher for the New Economics Foundation, explains, growth, materialism, and wealth "contains

121

within itself no limiting principle, while the environment in which it is placed is strictly limited." [4]

Alternative Economic Indicators

When I was growing up, my father once told me, as a metaphor for doing something that had no impact, that "X was as futile as peeing in the ocean." We now know, however, that six billion people peeing in the ocean would have a huge impact. And we know that we must exercise control over our past and continuing depletion and outright poisoning of the earth's resources. We need to design indicators that measure and evaluate on an annual basis the progress we are making in slowing the following onslaughts to the environment:

1. Tropical deforestation
2. Extinction of species
3. Global warming
4. Desertification
5. Wasteful levels of energy consumption
6. Ocean degradation

These indicators can be used as a basis of taxation and preservation of the environment. As Lester Brown, president of the Earth Policy Institute, wisely explains, "Taxes designed to incorporate in their prices the environmental costs of providing services enable the market to send the right signal . . . Environmental taxes can be used to represent the interests of future generations in situations where traditional economics simply discount the future." [5]

Furthermore, once we begin to break our thinking out of the conventional boxes of growth and profits as the only possible measurements of a healthy economy, all sorts of unforeseen benefits to society present themselves. For example, Peter Barnes—co-founder and former president of the socially responsible telephone company Working Assets—has written a book, *Who Owns the Sky*, in which he argues that "the sky belongs to all of us, and those who pollute it ought to pay the rest of us for the right to do so." [6] Again, here is a source of income for social and educational purposes that is crying out for implementation.

In the 1991 *State of the World* publication from the Worldwatch Institute, Sandra Postel and Christopher Flavin state that "Perhaps the single most powerful instrument for redirecting national economies toward environmental sustainability is taxation. Taxing products and activities that pollute, deplete, or otherwise degrade natural systems is a way of ensuring that environmental costs are taken into account in private decisions—whether to commute by car or bicycle, or to generate electricity from coal or sunlight. Each individual producer or consumer decides how to adjust to the higher costs: a tax on air emissions would lead some factories to add pollution controls, some to change their production processes, and others to redesign products so as to generate less waste. By raising a large proportion of revenue from such 'green taxes' and reducing income taxes or others to compensate, governments can help move economies swiftly onto a sustainable track." [7] For example, in 1996, at the local level, the city of Victoria, British Columbia, added a trash tax of $1.20 per bag of garbage, reducing its daily trash flow to 18 percent within one year. [8]

Lester Brown urges a process of shifting taxes—"Lowering income taxes while raising levies to get the market to tell the truth . . ." For in truth corporate profits often are achieved on the backs of public costs. Coal companies make profits by creating increased health costs resulting from acid rain and air pollution. Brown, in his latest study, *Plan B 2.0* (updated and expanded), cites numerous examples of nations that were able to achieve environment improvements through appropriate taxation. For example, "A four year plan adopted in Germany in 1999 systematically shifted taxes from labor to energy. By 2001, this plan had lowered fuel use by five percent. It had also accelerated growth in the renewable energy sector, creating some 45,500 jobs in the wind industry alone." [9]

Subsidizing our Own Destruction
In addition to using taxes to discourage ecologically destructive activities, we need to re-examine the use of government subsidies for the same purpose. Currently, governments around the world (see a 1997 Earth Council Study, *Subsidizing Unsustainable Development*) [10] are spending at least $700 billion to encourage the use of water, the burning of fossil fuels, the use of pesticides, and driving automobiles. As the Earth Council writers noticed,

"There is something unbelievable about the world spending hundreds of billions of dollars annually to subsidize its own destruction." [11]

Ecologist Norman Myers has established that more than $1.4 trillion is spent annually on such "perverse subsidies": that is, subsidies that actually harm the environment. [12] David Orr, in his 2004 study *The Last Refuge,* notes that, "In the United States specifically, estimates of subsidies for the automobile industry range from $400 billion to $700 billion. Levied as a tax on gasoline this amounts to something between $3.75 and $7 per gallon." [13]

There are three related solutions to this absurd practice. One would be simply to eliminate these subsidies altogether and spend the money on education and other social services. A second would be to shift the subsidies "to encourage environmentally constructive activities, such as investing in renewable energy, tree planting, family planning, and the education of young women in developing countries." [14] An obvious third would be to shift the $700 billion a year to a combination of the first and second solutions.

Green taxes can lead to more revenue for sustainable practices, for conservation, and for education of the public. It can be a win–win–win situation. What we have in place now is a system in which a few win big, temporarily, but, ultimately, everyone—even the rich—lose big. Lester Brown sums it up for all of us, "There is no middle path. Do we join together to build an economy that is sustainable? Or do we stay with our environmentally unsustainable economy until it declines? It is not a goal that can be compromised. One way or the other, the choice will be made by our generation. But it will affect life on earth for all generations to come." [15]

NOTES:

1 Michael Renner, "Moving Toward a Less Consumptive Economy," *State of the World: 2004.* Worldwatch Paper 167. (Washington, D.C.: Worldwatch Institute, 2004), pp. 96–119.

2 Ibid., p. 96.

3 Victor Vork, "Sustainable Development for the Second World." Worldwatch Paper 167. (Washington, D.C.: Worldwatch Institute, 2003), p. 43.

4 Victor Anderson, *Alternate Economic Indicators* (London and New York: Routledge, 1991), p. 5.

5 Lester Brown, *Eco-Economy: Building an Economy for the Earth* (New York: W. W. Norton &Co., 2001), p. 235.

6 Peter Barnes, *Who Owns the Sky?* (Washington, D.C.: Island Press, 2001), p. 8.

7 Sandra Postel and Christopher Flavin, "Reshaping the Global Economy," *State of the World: 2001*, ed. Lester Brown (Washington, D.C.: Worldwatch Institute, 2001), p. 181.

8 Brown, *Eco-Economy*, p. 211.

9 Brown, *Plan B 2.0: Rescuing a Planet under Stress and a Civilization in Trouble*, (New York: W. W. Norton & Co., 2006), p. 229.

10 Earth Council, Subsidizing Unsustainable Development. Discussed in Brown, *Eco Economy,* p. 240.

11 Ibid.

12 Norman Myers, *Perverse Subsidies* (Washington, D.C.: Island Press, 2000), pp. xvi–xvii.

13 David Orr, *The Last Refuge.* (Washington, D.C.: Island Press, 2004), p. 71.

14 Brown, *Eco-Economy*, p. 240.

15 Ibid., p. 276.

CHAPTER 18

Sin Taxes

I like to pay taxes, with them I buy civilization.
—Oliver Wendell Holmes, Jr.

As we have seen in the previous chapter the environmental costs of common consumer products often create external costs that everyone in society must bear. Consequently, we should not simply allow producers to calculate only their needs for profits when pricing their products; we should require them to take into account the social costs of their products to the general welfare of society as well. Under current conditions, although a given company may temporarily gain huge profits, often society as a whole loses.

Cigarettes have been the most obvious illustration of this fact. While cigarette companies made huge profits for decades, consumers of their products incurred huge medical costs and suffered family tragedies of enormous proportions. The Centers for Disease Control (CDC) issued a study that calculated the social costs of smoking cigarettes in the U.S. to be $7.18 a pack. Taxes on cigarettes may have the dual benefits of increasing revenue while lowering health expenses related to smoking— and reducing tragic deaths caused by lung cancer as well. As David Leonhardt writes, "Researchers already know that smokers are price-sensitive. Studies show that a 10 percent price increase produces about a 5 percent drop in smoking . . . taxes push people to take a step they had wanted to take before, but couldn't . . . The CDC said (in April of 2004) that the current level of cigarette taxes was not high enough to pay for the health problems caused by smoking. The beauty of cigarette taxation is that it is among the few public policies that can both raise revenue and cut costs." [1] In California, cigarette taxes have generated enough revenue to launch a new program of providing early childhood education for thousands of children.

I don't favor raising sales taxes because they are regressive in nature, but I believe we should make an exception in the case of products that cause great harm to individuals and to the larger community. Taxes (sometimes known as "sin taxes") that may help reduce addiction or limit the use of destructive products can benefit everyone. I do not for a moment believe in trying to legislate against an individual's freedom of choice, but I think we can try to encourage limits on choices that are clearly harmful to everyone.

Thus, I would advocate substantial tax increases on cigarettes, gasoline, gas-guzzling vehicles (SUVs in particular), guns and ammunition, and liquor. The social costs of each are huge, probably greater than any of us would like to imagine. Consider the three leading causes of death in America:

♦ Automobiles, which kill 117 Americans a day, or nearly 43,000 a year
♦ The flu, which kills 36,000 Americans a year
♦ Guns, which cause approximately 26,000 deaths in the U.S. per year (90 per day on the average during the 1990s)

In addition to seat belts and safety fixtures on guns, anything that reduces dependency on automobiles and easy access to guns will have huge social payoffs. For example, less reliance upon automobiles would not only reduce deaths, injuries and hospital costs, but would both improve air quality and reduce road rage caused by traffic jams. We should also note that SUVs (now 20 million in America) "spew up to 5.5 times as much smog-causing gases per mile as conventional cars." [2] Initially, the revenue generated by increased taxation on auto sales and gasoline might be used for rapid transit projects as well as school improvements. According to a recent Gallup poll, "Every year commuters idle away 3.6 billion hours and 5.7 billion gallons of gas stuck in traffic jams; congestion costs Americans $67 billion annually." If we were to apply revenue savings to improvements in our infrastructure, a wholly different scenario presents itself: "Every $1 billion of federal funds invested in highway infrastructure generates 47,500 jobs and $6.2 billion in economic activity." [3]

The same would apply to guns and ammunition. In addition to reducing the 26,000 deaths per year—about 71 per day, over eight times the Twin Tower deaths every year—we would not need to pay huge medical bills for attending to gunshot wounds. Emergency room units across the country are flooded with such victims. According to David Hemenway, "The direct medical costs of gunshot wounds were estimated at six million dollars per day in the 1990s. The mean medical costs of a gunshot injury is about seventeen thousand dollars and would be higher except that the medical costs for deaths at the scene are low. Half of these costs are borne directly by U.S. taxpayers; gun injuries are the leading cause of uninsured hospital stays in the United States. The best estimate of the cost of gun violence in America, derived from asking people how much they would pay to reduce it, is about one hundred billion dollars per year." [4]

The United States is one of the homicide capitals of the planet, although our bizarre fascination with guns clearly does nothing to make us safe. Substantial sales taxes imposed upon guns and ammunition would create a win–win–win situation: increased revenue for social and educational needs; lower health costs for gunshot victims; and fewer human tragedies. Twenty-six thousand deaths per year is another of those elephants in the living room that no one wants to discuss. Since abolition of guns seems politically impossible at this moment in history, perhaps taxation could lessen the harm they are now permitted to cause.

Sales or "sin" taxes do not destroy freedom of choice: they may, however, induce wiser choices. The point I am trying to make here is that increases in "sin taxes" can make available revenue for improving our cities and our schools.

NOTES:

1 David Leonhardt, "Economics," *New York Times*, April 14, 2004, p. C4.

2 Keith Bradsher, *High and Mighty* (New York: Public Affairs, 2002), p. xvii.

3 Heidi Pauken, "Hit the Road, George," *The American Prospect*, May 2004, pp. 1–8.

4 David Hemenway, *Private Guns, Public Health* (Ann Arbor: University of Michigan Press, 2004), p. 4.

The abyss doesn't divide us.
The abyss surrounds us.
—Symborksa

CHAPTER 19

The Progressive Social Security Tax

In my father's house are many mansions:
If it were not so, I would have told you.
—John XIV: 1

As an educator and now the executive director of a small foundation, I earn enough to pay full Social Security taxes (6.2 percent on my first $90,000 of salary), which amounts to $5,580. Billionaire Bill Gates pays this amount, as do Warren Buffett and Donald Trump. Each of us pays exactly the same amount: in other words, the Social Security tax is a flat tax. The $5,580 for someone earning $90,000 truly represents 6.2 percent of their total income; for billionaires, however, $5,580 represents considerably less than one percent of *their* total income. Although we decry the possibility of the future bankruptcy of our Social Security system and the disintegration of our schools, we have in place a governmentally imposed tax system that favors the rich, places a disproportionate burden on the less wealthy, and denies essential revenue to society as a whole.

Flat taxes are inherently unfair, and until the Reagan/Bush era, progressive taxes were considered equitable and appropriate. I recently came across a 1925 publication, *Income in the Various States: Its Sources and Distribution, 1919, 1920, and 1921,* by Maurice Levin and Willford Isbell King, a study published by a solid, middle-of-the-road economic research board. Levin and King contend:

> The view is widely held that, in a democratic country, a good government requires that the burden of taxation be felt by all citizens, for there can be no healthy interest in government, unless the majority of people feel that they contribute materially toward its support. However, it is also strongly contended that taxation should be graduated in accordance with the ability of the citizens to pay. [1]

That was in 1925. For decades afterward, simple principles of fairness ruled. Actually, "The idea of basing taxes on the ability to pay dates to ancient Athens," said Maureen B. Cavanaugh, a professor of tax law at Washington and Lee University, quoted in a recent *New York Times* article by David Cay Johnston. According to Johnston, "Athens was a tyranny when it had a flat tax . . . but a democracy flourished once taxes were based on one's ability to pay." [2] Nonetheless, since the corporate takeover of the American economy and the alliance between big business and government, that simple principle of fairness has been abandoned altogether.

Former senator from Illinois Paul Simon argues that "All income should be taxed for payments into the Social Security Retirement Trust Fund. Today, (2005), income up to only $90,000 is taxed. While the benefit payments are mildly progressive, the taxes are regressive. Most Americans pay more into Social Security than to the IRS." [3] Simon continues with a statement based on the fairness and good-of-the-commonwealth criteria of taxation:

> If you earn $1 million a year, your increased [Social Security] tax would be less than $57,000. You could afford that. And you would pay it knowing that you are helping insure a more secure old age for your children and grandchildren. [4]

Jim Hightower summarizes the situation accurately when he writes:

> There is one fix, however, that would guarantee the soundness of Social Security in perpetuity: raise the current $90,000 income cap so that the salaries, bonuses, stock gains, and other wealth of the elite are also subject to Social Security taxes—rather than keeping the burden solely on the wages of low-income and middle class working folks. [5]

Fairness dictates that the tax be progressive and that all income be taxed, not just wages.

The issue of funding Social Security leads us inevitably into the question of what kind of society we wish to build. Very few people can save enough money on their own to prepare for retirement and for life's twists, turns, and tragedies. Social Security wards off the many problems connected with old age, unemployment, illness and unforeseen family disasters. Ellen Frank points out that

> Virtually all people—certainly the 93 percent of U.S. households earning less than $150,000—would fare better collectively than they could individually. Programs that provide direct access to important goods and services—publicly financed education, recreation, health care, and pensions—reduce the inequities that follow inevitably from an entirely individualized economy. The vast majority of people are better off with high probability of a secure income and guaranteed access to key services such as health care than with the low-probability prospect of becoming rich. [6]

There is another way of looking at Social Security and the future of our nation. In 2004 Alan Greenspan acknowledged that the only way for poor people to traverse the growing divide between poverty and wealth is better education. Yet Greenspan was unwilling to back off from providing *unnecessary* tax cuts for the already wealthy. He and we all know that a healthy economy, improved paychecks, and a secure Social Security system are essential to create and support a decent educational system. Both Social Security and improved schools need proper funding, and the revenue for both must come from progressive tax systems in which everyone pays his or her fair share. A progressive Social Security tax would be an appropriate step.

NOTES:

1 Maurice Leven and Willford Isbell King, *Income in the Various States: Its Sources and Distribution 1919, 1920, 1921* (New York: National Bureau of Economic Research, Inc., 1925), p. 45.

2 David Cay Johnston, "A Taxation Policy to Make John Stuart Mill Weep," *New York Times*, April 18, 2004, p. 14.

3 As quoted in Neal Pierce, "Social Security Futures and School Funding: One Story?" *Nation*, April 29, 2004, page 242.

4 Ibid, p. 24.

5 Jim Hightower, "The Rich Should Pay Social Security Tax, Too," *Liberal Opinion Week,* June 7, 2004, p. 20.

6 Ellen Frank, "No More Savings! The Case for Social Wealth," *Dollars and Sense*, May/June 2004, p. 20.

> *The ruling ideas are the ideas of the ruling class.*
> —Karl Marx

CHAPTER 20

Random Acts of Taxation

We should be careful of each other,
we should be kind while there is still time.
—Philip Larkin

The various ideas outlined within these pages—truly progressive income and corporate taxes; wealth taxes; eco taxes; estate taxes; elimination of cheating and offshore tax shelters; sin taxes—are the most frequently discussed ideas for tax reform and revenue enhancement. Nevertheless, a few other, less mainstream ideas should perhaps be added to the mix. Rather than discuss them at length, I will simply mention them to whet an appetite or two, and to show that there are many ways we can raise the funds necessary to create high-quality schools for all our children and youth.

Impose a Surtax on High Incomes

In 2004 the Lieutenant Governor of Illinois, Pat Quinn, encouraged voters to support a referendum that would impose a three percent surtax on residents' adjusted gross income above $250,000 a year. [1] The plan, Mr. Quinn contended, would raise $1.5 billion annually. Half, he proposed, would go to schools.

Impose a Progressive Consumption Tax

A second solution to the problem of the tax burden having been shifted onto the backs of working-class people is to reduce payroll taxes and institute a progressive consumption tax. The tax would be levied not on individual purchases—which would be regressive—but on an individual's total spending for the year. Ted Halstead, president and CEO of the New American Foundation, and Maya MacGuiness, director of the Foundation's Fiscal Policy Program, suggest that "Each year taxpayers would calculate their total income, subtract their total savings and pay taxes on the difference. The first say $25,000 of consumption would be tax free, and from there the taxes would be progressive rather than flat. The more you spend and the less you have saved, the higher your tax would be." [2] As former U.S. Senator Gary Hart observes: "While consuming our wealth, we depend on the investments of foreigners to finance our debt and even our defense, sending much of the profits from our own productivity abroad." After a brief Clintonian interlude of public surpluses and debt reduction, President Bush has spearheaded a return to "massive debts and massive borrowing from both foreigners and future generations." [3] However, a progressive tax on consumption would encourage savings and investment, and would help us to reduce deficits and reduce waste and pollution—as noted in Chapter 17.

Impose a Consumption Tax on Luxury Items

As the economist Robert Frank and others have written, a tax on luxury items could be structured so as to affect luxury spending only. Consumption up to a certain level—that needed to cover necessities—would not be taxed, nor would money put into savings. Consumption beyond those expenditures would be taxed at a progressive rate, with the rate rising with the amount of luxury spending. [4]

Raise Taxes on Dividends and Capital Gains

As Alan Sloan writes, "Come on, already, income is income. Taxing dividends and capital gains as regular income would still leave them [the beneficiaries] with a significant advantage over salary—you don't pay Social Security and Medicare tax on investments. It's wrong on both fairness and fiscal grounds to give capital income a subsidized ride while charging salary-earners full fare." [5] Making this change would add billions of dollars to the federal budget—billions that could be spent on our schools and other areas of need.

Require Delinquents to Pay Back Taxes Before Receiving Further Federal Contracts

Here is a novel idea: let's *not* provide federal contractors new contracts and payments until they pay the government what they owe in back taxes. According to Norm Coleman, "Some 33,000 federal contractors together owe the Internal Revenue Service more than $3.3 billion in back taxes." [6]

Reform Laws Like California's Proposition 13
My next-door neighbor pays $12,000+ a year in property taxes; I pay $3000. My wife and I bought our home before Proposition 13 (approved in 1978); he bought his later. Tough luck for him—and for all the rest of us in California who have seen our social services and school systems decline. The solution is simple and obvious: assess property taxes on current valuation rather than one percent of an arbitrary and obsolete base of 1975–76. The current system is poorly designed and patently unfair, and results in a disastrous loss of income for states that employ such approaches.

Change Payroll Tax Exemptions
A January 27, 2005 Congressional study cited by Edmund Andrews claimed that the federal government "could raise $164 billion over 10 years by changing the laws that exempt from payroll taxes for Social Security and Medicare, a variety of fringe benefits, including employer-paid health insurance and child care assistance." [7] The savings of $16.4 billion per year could fund a variety of educational needs in our nation's inner cities.

Eliminate Tax Deductions for Advertising
If ever there was a silly form of corporate welfare, surely corporate tax deductions for advertising is it. In her study *The Overspent American* Juliet B. Schor explains, "Ad expenditures have skyrocketed in recent years and now stand at more than $2,000 per family. These expenditures are fully subsidized by taxpayers: advertising costs are deductible from corporate profits. If this write-off were revoked, it's likely there would be fewer ads, which nearly everyone but Madison Avenue probably agrees would be a good thing. (Sixty-five percent of the public already agree with such an idea, and 80 percent believe that prime-time advertising should be limited.) It's time to get this giveaway on the congressional docket." [8]

The 2% Solution
Matthew Miller has come up with a seemingly bipartisan solution to many social and educational problems, which he calls "The 2% Solution." He proposes budgeting "two cents on the dollar [which] means two percent of our $11 trillion national income (gross domestic product or GDP) that is $220 billion a year." [9] He would then take the $220 billion and spend it as follows:

Increased salaries for teachers	$30
Health care for everyone in the USA	$80
A generously funded educational voucher system	$2
Universal preschool	$10
Construction and repairs in public schools	$10
Wage subsidies for low-income workers	$85
"Patriot dollars"	$3
Total	$ 220 billion

Miller also proposes some additional sources of revenue savings:

1. Stop giving unjustified subsidies to big corporations—he proposes cutting only "25 percent of corporate welfare as we know it." Projected savings: $25 billion.

2. Stop subsidizing extra health care for Americans who already have good coverage and use the money to help subsidize basic coverage for those who don't. Projected savings: $35 billion.

3. Cancel a portion of President Bush's tax relief for America's highest earners. Projected savings: $70 billion.

These are but three of his seven proposals. They confirm my thesis that the money and the resources are there to solve our educational and social problems. Priorities are the real issue.

Conclusion
If we are to preserve democracy rather than slide irreversibly into oligarchy, we urgently need radically new thinking. Carl Upchurch wrote a wonderful book describing his life in a ghetto and gave the book the disturbing title *Convicted in the Womb*. [10] Carl managed to climb out of the dire circumstances of his environment; most children do not, and as

a society we fail them. We need to reallocate resources, create opportunity, and rebuild neighborhoods and schools, all of which will require revenue. Revenue. Not cuts in taxes, not cuts in services, but revenue!

NOTES:

1 Sean Cavanagh, "Taxing Plan," *Education Week*, March 3, 2004, p. 15.

2 Ted Halstead and Maya MacGuineas, "A Tax Plan for Kerry," *Liberal Opinion Week*, June 7, 2004, p. 20.

3 Gary Hart, *The Fourth Power* (Oxford, UK: Oxford University Press, 2004), p. 77.

4 David Callahan, *The Cheating Culture* (Orlando: Harcourt Inc., 2004), p. 279.

5 Alan Sloan, "Why Your Tax Cut Doesn't Add Up," *Newsweek*, April 12, 2004, pp.41–47.

6 Norm Coleman, *New York Times,* June 2005.

7 Edmund L. Andrews, "Congressional Study Notes Ways to Collect Billions More in Taxes," *New York Times*, January 28, 2005, p. A15.

8 Juliet B. Schor, *The Overspent American* (New York: HarperPerennial, 1998), p. 165.

9 Matt Miller, *The 2% Solution: Fixing America's Problems in Ways Liberals and Conservatives Can Love* (New York: Public Affairs, 2003), p. ix.

10 Carl Upchurch, *Convicted in the Womb* (New York: Bantam Books, 1996).

CHAPTER 21

Penultimate Conclusion: Ending Class Divisiveness

*The middle class and working poor are told that what's happening
to them is the consequence of Adam Smith's 'Invisible Hand.'
This is a lie. What's happening to them is the direct consequence of
corporate activism, intellectual propaganda, the rise of a religious
orthodoxy that in its hunger for government subsidies has made an
idol of power, and a string of political decisions favoring the powerful
and the privileged who bought the political system right out from under us.*
—Bill Moyers

The deadliest form of violence is poverty.
—Gandhi

It is difficult to avoid the conclusion that America is experiencing a growing class divisiveness in which intentionally (or even unintentionally) the wealthy minority is beguiling, exploiting, and abusing the lower and even the middle classes. A spate of well researched books has been published in the past few decades illuminating this phenomenon. In fact, several of the book titles are themselves revealing:

David Broder, *Democracy Derailed*
Noam Chomsky, *Class Warfare*
Chuck Collins and Felice Yeskel, *Economic Apartheid in America*
Sheldon Danziger and Peter Gottschalk, *America Unequal*
Thom Hartman, *Unequal Protection: The Rise of Corporate
Dominance and the Theft of Human Rights*
Charles M. Kelly, *Class War in America: How Economic and Political
Conservatives Are Exploiting Low- and Middle-Income Americans*
Mickey Kraus, *The End of Equality*
Jonathan Kozol, *The Shame of a Nation: The Restoration of Apart-heid
Schooling in America.*

Charles Lewis and Bill Allison, *The Cheating of America: How Tax Avoidance and Evasion By the Super Rich Are Costing the Country Billions—And What You Can Do About It*
Michael Parenti, *Democracy for the Few*

This list could be expanded for many pages, with similar variations on the theme of the rich getting richer and more powerful, the poor sinking into an inextricable morass, and the middle class just barely hanging on.

This phenomenon is, of course, not just an American issue. William K. Tabb, author and professor of economics at Queens College, cites some additional shocking realities—unless, of course, we have gradually become too numb to be shocked:

1. The world's richest 20 percent now receive 86 percent of the world's gross domestic product, the poorest 20 percent only one percent, and the middle 60 percent just 13 percent.
2. The world's richest three *people* have assets greater than the combined output of the 48 poorest *countries!*
3. The world's richest two hundred people saw their incomes *double* between 1994 and 1998, to more than a trillion dollars. [1]

These facts are mirrored in America, which also has seen a dramatic and almost unbelievable widening and stratifying of the gap between rich and poor over the past few decades. (And let's not forget that the United States ranks last in foreign aid among major industrialized nations.) [2]

The relevance for this book is clear: our schools, particularly schools in inner-city, urban and poor rural neighborhoods are suffering great deprivations while public and private schools that serve mainly the affluent are flourishing. Just a coincidence or is it the result of institutionalized and unexamined classism? Whatever it is, it is not benign. A country that prides itself on its morality, equality, and sense of fairness is clearly moving in a contradictory direction: aristocracy and oligarchy.

The ten books mentioned earlier all present startling statistics to illustrate the direction in which the United States is headed. Here are but a few:

1. The U.S. financial wealth of the top one percent now exceeds the combined household wealth of the bottom 95 percent.

2. The share of the nation's after-tax income received by the top one percent nearly doubled from 1979 to 1997.
3. The top 20 percent of U.S. households now claim 49.2 percent of the national income, while the bottom 20 percent receives 3.6 percent.
4. The average income of the top 0.1 percent of Americans was $1.2 million in 1980; by 2002 it was 2 ½ times this at $3 million! No other income group rose nearly as fast. The share of the nation's income for the bottom 90% fell! from 1980 to 2002. [3]

Class conflict, growing disparities of wealth, racial conflict, class warfare. James Gilligan, M.D., formerly Director of the Center for the Study of Violence at Harvard Medical School, speaks of a caste system in America in which "blacks have always been there to occupy a position lower in the social scale than even the poorest whites." [4] This positioning, Gilligan argues, enables poor whites to let themselves "be distracted from paying attention to how badly they are being discriminated against by the class system, by the fact that there is always a group they can look down upon in the caste system . . . this in turn buys peace for the rich, who can continue to monopolize most of the nation's wealth and income without having to be bothered by any significant threats to their privileges from either of the two groups they are exploiting (all blacks, and poor and middle class whites)." [5]

A third group, Latinos, must now be added to the list of those exploited. In 2003, the Census Bureau estimated that 35.9 million Americans had incomes below the poverty line, and that since 2000 poverty has risen among most racial groups: "Hispanics account for most of the increase in poverty." [6] Consequently, in segregated districts and inner-city schools across the country, we see people of color receiving the short end of national resources and funding.

The caste system is even more apparent when we examine the forgotten sufferers of our country: Native Americans. The quality of life and schools on Indian reservations continues to be a national disgrace. But since no president in recent memory has even acknowledged their existence, much less their social and economic deprivations, reform in this area is pretty much off the radar screen.

For generation after generation these disparities have continued, except for one recent and dramatic change: since 1979 they have become worse. The disparities of wealth between the top 20 percent of the population and the remaining 80 percent have increased, and the disparities between the top 5 percent and the bottom 20 percent have become nothing less than shocking. Consider the following: [7]

- A survey of multibillion-dollar corporations found them paying CFOs more than $3 million a year, top legal officers $2.2 million.
- According to the Congressional Budget Office, between 1979 and 1997 the richest one percent of American families (incomes of at least $677,900 in 1997) had their incomes double. The income of families in the middle grew by 10 percent while the lowest 20 percent actually fell.
- *Business Week* recently listed 10 executives with jobs below CEO who received more than $29 million each in 2003.
- Also, a December 2004 study by the National Low Income Housing Coalition reported that "In only four of the nation's 3,066 counties can someone who works full-time and earns the federal minimum wage afford to pay rent and utilities of a one-bedroom apartment." [8]

It is difficult to escape the suspicion that this is intentional and systematic.

The operation of class divisions can be clearly witnessed in our educational system, where poor and low-income children receive substantially fewer resources and therefore poorly functioning schools. Our neglectful or mean-spirited policies manifest themselves in the funding of special education, where children of color and children with disabilities suffer. In 1975, Congress passed the Individuals with Disabilities Education Act (IDEA), mandating that 40 percent of the additional costs of special education would be paid by the federal government. Today, however, the federal government pays only 17 percent of the costs. In fact, Senator James M. Jeffords writes: "The chronic underfunding of special education is inexcusable. It was a major factor in my decision to leave the Republican Party in 2001 and declare myself an Independent." [9] Jeffords has proposed boosting special education funding by $2.5 billion each year until 2007, which would bring it up to the 40 percent level. So far his calls have fallen on deaf ears.

When the economic playing field is dramatically uneven to begin with—and becoming more and more uneven—education is the only way of leveling the field for poor and low-income students. But when the education they are offered is itself inequitable, then the game is virtually over before it has begun. This is not how a democracy is supposed to function, nor can a democracy so survive.

The class separations are now thoroughly politicized. As Gar Alperovitz notes: "A recent study found that 81 percent of individuals who donate at least $200 to congressional campaigns make over $100,000 per year; 46 percent make at least $250,000. Those among the bottom fifth vote less . . . and are only one-tenth as likely to make any form of campaign contribution as those in the top one-tenth." [10] Those who contribute receive tax cuts; those who don't find their children receive cuts in educational services. It is the golden rule: "those with the gold rule." Michael Lind puts it equally bluntly: "From organizations of the private sector, protected by the concentric moats of alumni preference, college tuition, professional licensing and pro-managerial state law, the white overclass dominates U.S. politics." [11]

Another disturbing dimension to the class divisiveness in America is the despair and hopelessness enveloping lower-income citizens, a despair reflected by their non-participation in the political process. We can, of course, leap to the conclusion that "it's their own fault if they don't vote." Certainly on one level this is so. But after decades of neglect and the realization that politicians in both parties place poverty and its remediation at the bottom of their list of priorities, it is easy to see why despair takes hold. The November 2004 issue of *National Geographic* published a chart showing how the United States compares to other countries in its voting patterns: [12]

HOW THE U.S. COMPARES

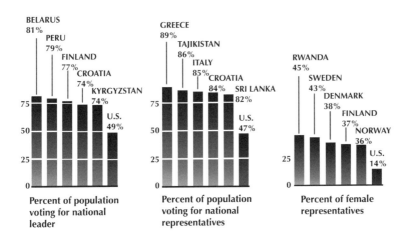

Percent of population
voting for national
leader

Percent of population
voting for national
representatives

Percent of female
representatives

Other studies show that the 50 percent who do not vote are primarily lower-income and minority voters who have given up believing that the political system is at all interested in their fate.

When we combine the voting dropout rate with the school dropout rate in inner cities, we see a clearer correlation: less- well-educated people show up disproportionately in the growing statistics of the incarcerated, homeless, unemployed and the disenfranchised. Does this matter? Certainly it seems not to matter to those who enjoy the blessings and powers of our society. But in the final analysis it drags us all down. Thomas Jefferson wrote: "If a nation expects to be ignorant and free, it expects what never has been and never will be." Class divisiveness and disparities are a cancer eating away the soul of America. Education is the antidote—but it must be properly funded education.

Which brings us back to the premise of this book: achieving educational quality and redressing inequality costs money. The money is now unfairly distributed and mainly controlled at the top. The solution seems clear: redistribute resources, funds, and hence opportunities to benefit our schools, our children, and our future.

NOTES:

1 William K. Tabb, *Unequal Partners: A Primer on Globalization* (New York: The New Press, 2002), p. 206.

2 Editorial, "Tight With A Buck," *Los Angeles Times*, January 23, 2005, editorial page.

3 David Cay Johnston, "Richest Are Leaving Even the Rich Behind," *New York Times*, June 5, 2005, p.1.

4 James Gilligan, *Violence: Reflections on a National Epidemic* (New York: Vantage Books, 1996), p. 199.

5 Ibid.

6 Robert J. Samuelson, "The Changing Face of Poverty," *Newsweek*, October 18, 2004, p. 50.

7 Vince Beiser, "Rise of the Corporate Plutocrats," *Los Angeles Times Magazine*, October 17, 2004.

8 "Study Finds Gap in Wages and Housing Costs," *New York Times*, December 25, 2004, p. A12.

9 Daniel Losen and Gary Orfield, *Racial Inequity in Special Education* (Cambridge, MA: Harvard Education Press, 2002), p. x.

10 Gar Alperovitz, *America Beyond Capitalism* (Hoboken, NJ: John Wiley & Sons, 2005), p. 50.

11 Michael Lind, *The Next American Nation* (New York: The Free Press, 1995), p. 156.

12 Karen E. Lange, "A Vote for Democracy," *National Geographic*, November 2004, Geographica Section.

> *We face the possibility of a new feudalism, in which most Americans provide personal services for the rich few*
> —Michael Lind

CHAPTER 22

Conclusion: *We* Could *Do It*

There is nothing in man's plight that his vision,
if he cared to cultivate it, could not alleviate.
The challenge is to see what could be done,
and then have the heart and the resolution
to attempt it.

—George Kennan

The tragic yet intriguing reality is that the United States *could* afford to implement the reforms, curriculum enrichment programs and structural changes that would make education adequate—even excellent—for all students. We *could* afford to offer higher salaries that would attract and retain first-rate teachers. We *could* afford to design and build new model schools and to renovate and refurbish our existing substandard facilities across the country. We *could* afford to offer comprehensive and enriched curricula for all our children and youth; we *could* afford to do all this and more. The funds are there. The resources are available. Lacking are both leadership and will on the part of the people who have the power and control the funds, as well as a properly motivated, enfranchised, and insistent public sector. Unfortunately, we have been so indoctrinated by the dominant corporate powers that we (the general public) believe the way things are is the way things must be.

If we truly believed education is fundamental to democracy, then we would fund it properly. How? Through any of the ideas discussed in this and like-minded publications. Each is feasible. None is prohibited by God or nature, but simply ignored or dismissed out of hand. Why? Because the goal of power is more power, not redistribution of wealth or equalization of opportunity. Remember that the ideas outlined in this book are designed to create high-quality education for every child in America and to bring equity into the educational arena so that every child flourishes. This is not un-American; it is not unpatriotic. It is simply fair, ethical, and moral.

First of all, we need to disabuse ourselves of the notion that taxation is evil. It is not. It is, however, portrayed as such by those who do not want to be taxed: the rich and the super-rich. Taxation is the main source of government revenue. It is a means of leveling the playing field and investing in equality of opportunity. Second, we need to acknowledge that we Americans are not taxed at nearly as high a rate as are taxpayers in other countries. In fact, of the 20 largest countries in the world, the U.S. has the *lowest* ratio of taxes to gross domestic product and we provide our citizens with fewer services than many of the other industrialized countries. [1] Perhaps, as *New York Times* columnist Thomas Friedman recently explained, there would probably be less revulsion [against taxes] if the word "services" replaced "taxes." Since all people, rich or poor, have access to public services (unlike private wealth), slogans like "Read my lips; no new services" might be sneered at rather than cheered.

We do not tax ourselves excessively, not even reasonably. As we routinely complain that we do not have enough funds to rebuild our inner cities, provide housing and health care for all our citizens, and provide a superb education for every child, the disconnect is easy to see. We do have resources and revenue possibilities; we simply need the courage to harvest these funds.

Where the funds are:

Item	Estimated Savings
Restore progressive corporate taxes	180 billion
Cut corporate welfare, i.e., subsidies	1.1 trillion
Cut defense spending by 15 percent	60 billion
Eliminate offshore tax shelters	82 billion
Require foreign multinationals to pay U.S. taxes	30 billion
Repeal tax cuts (return top one percent to 1977 levels)	200 billion
Impose estate taxes, with exemptions of $5 million	20 billion
Impose a wealth tax	55 billion
Hire more IRS investigators to cut tax cheating	70 billion
Increase taxes on capital gains/dividends	billions
Eco taxes:	
impose taxes like Germany's	20 billion
eliminate ecologically destructive subsidies	20 billion
"Sin taxes"	billions
A "Tobin Tax" on international transactions (10 percent)	54 billion
The 6 percent progressive Social Security tax	billions

"The 2% Solution"   200 billion

Random acts of taxation (a wild guess)   100 billion

Reform CEO pay   10 billion

 Delete stock options as deductions

Total funds available to rebuild America (annual basis): <u>Trillions</u>

NOTES:

1 William G. Gale, "Americans May Gripe But Taxes Are Low," *International Herald Tribune,* March 2, 1999, p.9.

Books

Abramovitz, Mimi. 1996. *Under Attack, Fighting Back: Women and Welfare in the United States.* New York: Monthly Review Press.

Ackerman, Bruce & Anne Alstott. 1999. *The Stakeholder Society.* New Haven, CT: Yale University Press.

Adams, Charles. 1993. *For Good and Evil: The Impact of Taxes on the Course of Civilization.* Silver Spring, MD: Madison Books.

Alperovitz, Gar. 2005. *America Beyond Capitalism. Hoboken, NJ: John Wiley & Sons.*

Alterman, Eric & Mark Green. 2004. *The Book on Bush: How George W. (Mis)Leads America.* New York: Viking.

Altman, Daniel. 2004. *Neoconomy: George Bush's Revolutionary Gamble with America's Future.* New York: Public Affairs.

Anderson, Victor. 1991. *Alternative Economic Indicators.* New York: Routledge.

Andreas, Joe. 2002. *Addicted to War.* Oakland, CA: AK Press.

Athanasiou, Tom. 1996. *Divided Planet: The Ecology of Rich and Poor.* Boston: Little Brown and Company.

Bakan, Joel. 2004. *The Corporation: The Pathological Pursuit of Profit and Power.* New York: Free Press.

Barlett, Donald L. & James B. Steele, 1994. *America: Who Really Pays The Taxes?* New York: A Touchstone Book.

Barnes, Peter. 2001. *Who Owns the Sky?* Washington, D.C.: Island Press.

Begala, Paul. 2002. *It's Still the Economy, Stupid: George W. Bush, The GOP's CEO.* New York: Simon and Schuster.

Behrman, J.R., and N. Stacey. 1997. *The Social Benefits of Education.* Ann Arbor: Michigan University Press.

Berman, Marshall. 1999. *Adventures in Marxism.* New York: Verso.

Birnbaum, Jeffrey H., Alan S. Murray. 1987. *Showdown at Gucci Gulch: Lawmakers, Lobbyists, and the Unlikely Triumph of Tax Reform.* New York: Random House.

Blau, Joe. 1992. *The Visible Poor: Homelessness in the United States.* New York: Oxford University Press.

Bradford, David F. 2000. *Taxation, Wealth, and Saving.* Cambridge, MA: The MIT Press.

Bradsher, Keith. 2002. *High and Mighty.* New York: Public Affairs.

Broder, David S. 2000. *Democracy Derailed: Initiative Campaigns and the Power of Money.* New York: A Harvest Book.

Brown, Lester R. 2001. *Eco-Economy.* New York: W.W. Norton & Co.

_____. Ed. 1991. *State of the World.* Washington, D.C.: Worldwatch Institute.

_____. 2006. *Plan B 2.0: Rescuing a Planet Under Stress and a Civilization in Trouble.* New York: W.W. Norton & Co.

Burtless, G. 1996. *Does Money Matter?* Washington, DC: Brookings Press.

Callahan, David. 2004. *The Cheating Culture.* Orlando, FL: Harcourt Inc.

Calleo, David P. 1992. *The Bankrupting of America.* New York: Avon Books.

Carroll, Stephen J., et al. 2005. *California's K–12 Public Schools.* Santa Monica, CA: Rand Education.

Carter, Graydon. 2004. *What We've Lost.* New York: Farrar, Straus and Giroux.

Chomsky, Noam. 1996. *Class Warfare.* Monroe, ME: Common Courage Press.

Chua, Amy. 2003. *World on Fire.* New York: Doubleday.

Clawson, Dan, Alan Neustadtl & Denise Scott. 1992. *Money Talks: Corporate PACS and Political Influences.* New York: Basic Books.

Collins, Chuck and Felice Yeskel. 2000. *Economic Apartheid in America.* New York: The New Press.

Conant, James B. 1961. *Slums and Suburbs.* New York: A Signet Book.

Conason, Joe. 2003. *Big Lies: The Right-Wing Propaganda Machine and How it Distorts the Truth.* New York: Thomas Dunne Books.

Coons, John; William N. Clune; and Stephen Sugarman. 1970. *Private Wealth and Public Education.* Cambridge, MA: Harvard University Press.

Crosby, Brian. 2001. *The $100,000 Teacher.* Sterling, VA; Capital Books.

Cuban, Larry & Dorothy Shipps, eds. 2000. *Reconstructing the Common Good in Education.* Stanford, CA: Stanford University Press.

Cummins, Paul. 2002. *Keeping Watch: Reflections on American Culture, Education and Politics.* 1ˢᵗ Books Library: www.1stBooks.com.

Cummins, Paul & Anna. 1998. *For Mortal Stakes: Solutions for Schools and Society.* New York: Peter Lang.

Cummins, Paul & Anna & Emily. 2004. *Proceed With Passion: Engaging Students in Meaningful Education.* Los Angeles, CA: Red Hen Press.

Danaher, Kevin. 2001. *10 Reasons to Abolish the IMF and World Bank.* New York: Seven Stories Press.

_____. 1996. *Corporations Are Gonna Get Your Mama.* Monroe, ME: Common Courage Press.

Danziger, Sheldon and Peter Gottschalk. 1995. *America Unequal.* New York: Russell Sage Foundation.

Davidson, James Dale & Lord William Rees-Mogg. 1997. *The Sovereign Individual.* New York: Simon & Schuster.

Donnelly, David, Janice Fine, and Ellen S. Miller. 2001. *Are Elections for Sale?* Boston: Beacon Press.

Donnelly, David, Janice Fine, and Ellen S. Miller. 1999. *Money and Politics: Financing Our Elections Democratically.* Boston: Beacon Press.

Duncan, Cynthia M. 1999. *Worlds Apart: Why Poverty Persists in Rural America.* New Haven, CT: Yale University Press.

Ehrenreich, Barbara. 2001. *Nickel and Dimed*. New York: Avon Books.

Esquith, Rafe. 2003. *There Are No Shortcuts*. New York: Pantheon Books.

Finn, Chester E. Jr., Bruno V. Manno & Greg Vanourek. 2000. *Charter Schools in Action*. Princeton, NJ: Princeton University Press.

Firestone, William A., Margaret E. Goeatz & Gary Natriello. 1997. *The Struggle for Fiscal Reform and Educational Change in New Jersey.* New York: Teachers College Press.

Fishman, Leo. Ed. 1966. *Poverty Amid Affluence*. New Haven: Yale University Press.

Flynt, Larry. 2004. *Sex, Lies and Politics: The Naked Truth*. New York: Kensington Books.

Frank, Ellen. 2004. *The Raw Deal*. Boston: Beacon Press.

Frank, Robert H. & Philip J. Cook. 1995. *The Winner-Take-All Society.* New York: The Free Press.

Frank, Thomas. 2000. *One Market Under God*. New York: Doubleday.

Franken, Al. 2003. *Lies and the Lying Liars Who Tell Them*. New York: Dutton.

Freire, Paulo. 1997. *Pedagogy of the Heart*. New York: Continuum.

Friedman, Benjamin M. 2005. *The Moral Consequences of Economic Growth*. New York: Alfred A. Knopf.

Galbraith, John Kenneth. 2004. *The Economics of Innocent Fraud: Truth for Our Time*. Boston: Houghton Mifflin Company.

Gates. Sr., William R. & Chuck Collins. 2002. *Wealth and Our Commonwealth: Why Americans Should Tax Accumulated Fortunes*. Boston: Beacon Press.

Giecek, Tamara Sober. 2000. *Teaching Economics as if People Mattered*. Boston: United for a Fair Economy.

Gilligan, James. 1996. *Violence: Reflections on a National Epidemic*. New York: Vintage Books.

Glickman, Carl. Ed. 2004. *Letters to the Next President: What We Can Do About the Real Crisis in Public Education*. New York: Teachers College Press, Columbia University.

Greenbaum, Howard. 1990. *Free Elections???* Kelseyville, CA: P.V. Goldsmith Publishing Company.

Greider, William. 1998. *One World, Ready or Not: The Manic Logic of Global Capitalism.* New York: Touchstone Books.

_____. 1998. *Fortress America: The American Military and the Consequences of Peace.* New York: Public Affairs.

Harrington, Michael. 1962. *The Other America: Poverty in the United States.* New York: Penguin Books.

Hart, Gary. 2004. *The Fourth Power: A Grand Strategy for the U.S. in the Twenty-First Century.* New York: Oxford University Press.

Hartman, Thom. 2002. *Unequal Protection: The Rise of Corporate Dominance and the Theft of Human Rights.* New York: St. Martin's Press.

Hedeman, Ed. 2003. (5th Ed.) *War Tax Resistance.* New York: War Resisters League.

Heintz, James, Nancy Folbre, and The Center for Popular Economics. 2000. *Field Guide to the U.S. Economy.* New York: The New Press.

Hemenway, David. 2004. *Private Guns, Public Health.* Ann Arbor: University of Michigan Press.

Henderson, Hazel. 1996. *Creating Alternative Futures.* West Hartford, CT: Kumarian Press.

Herbert, Bob. 2005. *Promises Betrayed: Waking Up from the American Dream.* New York: Henry Holt and Company.

Herman, Jerry J. and Janice L. Herman. 1997. *School-Based Budgets: Getting, Spending and Accounting.* Lancaster, PA: Tehomic Publications.

Hightower, Jim. 2003. *Thieves in High Places.* New York: Viking.

_____. 2004. *Let's Stop Beating Around the Bush.* New York: Viking.

Hodgson, Godfrey. 2004. *More Equal Than Others.* Princeton: Princeton University Press.

House, Ernest R. 1998. *Schools for Sale: Why Free Market Policies Won't Improve America's Schools and What Will.* New York: Teachers College Press.

Huffington, Arianna. 2003. *Pigs at the Trough: How Corporate Greed and Political Corruption Are Undermining America.* New York: Crown Publishers.

_____. 2004. *Fanatics and Fools: The Game Plan for Winning Back America.* New York: Hyperion.

Ivins, Molly & Lou Dubose. 2003. *Bushwhacked: Life in George W. Bush's America.* New York: Vintage Books.

Johnson, Chalmers. 2004. *The Sorrows of Empire: Militarism, Secrecy, and the End of Republic.* New York: Metropolitan Books.

Johnston, David Cay. 2003. *Perfectly Legal: The Covert Campaign to Rig Our Tax System to Benefit the Super Rich – and Cheat Everybody Else.* New York: Portfolio.

Karp, Stan, et. al. 1997. *Funding for Justice.* Milwaukee, WI: Rethinking Schools.

Kelly, Charles M. 2000. *Class War in America.* Santa Barbara, CA: Fithian Press.

Keister, Lisa A. 2000. *Wealth in America: Trends in Wealth Inequality.* Cambridge, MA: Cambridge University Press.

Kohn, Alfie. 1999. *The Schools Our Children Deserve.* New York: Houghton Mifflin Company.

Kotlikoff, Lawrence J. & Scott Burns. 2004. *The Coming Generational Storm.* Cambridge, MA: MIT Press.

Korton, David C. 1955. *When Corporations Rule the World.* West Hartford, CT: Kumarian Press.

Kozol, Jonathan. 1995. *Amazing Grace: The Lives of Children and the Conscience of A Nation.* New York: Crown Publishers.

_____. 1991. *Savage Inequalities: Children in America's Schools.* New York: HarpersPerennnial.

_____. 2005. *The Shame of the Nation.* New York: Crown Publishers.

Kraus, Mickey. 1992. *The End of Equality.* New York: Basic Books.

Krugman, Paul. 2003. *The Great Unraveling: Losing Our Way in the New Century.* New York: W.W. Norton & Co.

_____. 1994. *The Age of Diminished Expectations.* Cambridge, MA: M.I.T. Press.

Ladd, Helen F., Rosemary Chalk, and Janet S. Hansen, eds. 1999. *Equity and Adequacy in Education Finance.* Washington, D.C.: National Academy Press.

Ladd, Helen F. & Janet S. Hanson, Editors. 2001. *Making Money Matter: Financing America's Schools.* Washington, D.C.: National Academy Press.

Lapham, Lewis H. 1988. *Money and Class in America.* New York: Weidenfeld & Nicolson.

LeRoy, Greg. 1995. *No More Candy Store.* Washington, D.C.: Grassroots Policy Project.

Leven, Maurice & Willford Isbell King. 1925. *Income in the Various States: Its Sources and Distribution 1919, 1920, 1921.* New York: National Bureau of Economic Research, Inc.

Lewis, Charles and Bill Allison. 2002. *The Cheating of America.* New York: Harper Collins Books.

Lewis, Charles. 1996. *The Buying of the President.* New York: Avon Books.

Lieberman, Myron. 1960. *Future of Public Education.* Chicago, IL: University of Chicago Press. 1962.

Lind, Michael. 1995. *The Next American Nation.* New York: The Free Press.

Losen, Daniel J. & Gary Orfield. 2002. *Racial Inequality in Special Education.* Cambridge, MA: Harvard University Press.

Martin, Cathie J. 1991. *Shifting the Burden.* Chicago: The University of Chicago Press.

Martin, Hans Peter & Harold Schumann. 1997. *The Global Trap: Globalization and the Assault on Prosperity and Democracy.* London, UK: Zed Books, Ltd.

Miller, Matthew. 2003. *The 2% Solution.* New York: Public Affairs.

Mitchell, Lawrence E. 2001. *Corporate Irresponsibility: America's Newest Export.* New Haven, CT: Yale University Press.

Moore, Michael. 2003. *Dude, Where's My Country?* New York: Warner Books.

Myers, Norman. 2000. *Perverse Subsidies.* Washington, D.C.: Island Press.

Nader, Ralph. 2000. *Cutting Corporate Welfare.* New York: Seven Stories Press.

Odden, Allan R. 1992. *Rethinking School Finance.* San Francisco: Jossey-Bass Publishers.

Orfield, Gary & Chungmei Lee. 2005. *Racial Transformation and the Changing Nature of Segregation.* Harvard University: Civil Rights Project.

Orr, David. 2004. *The Last Refuge: Patriotism, Politics, and the Environment in an Age of Terror.* Washington, D.C.: Island Press.

Ouchi, William G. 2003. *Making Schools Work.* New York: Simon & Schuster.

Palast, Greg. 2002. *The Best Democracy Money Can Buy.* New York: Plume.

Parenti, Michael. 1995. *Democracy for the Few.* (6th Ed.) New York: St. Martin's Press.

Perkins, John. 2004. *Confessions of an Economic Hit Man.* San Francisco: Berrett-Koehler Publishers.

Perlo, Ellen, Stanley, and Arthur, eds. 2003. *People vs. Profits: Columns of Victor Perlo: 1961–1999, Volume I, The Home Front.* New York: International Publishers.

Perrow, Charles. 2002. *Organizing America: Wealth, Power, and the Origins of Corporate Capitalism.* Princeton, NJ: Princeton University Press.

Philips, Kevin. 1990. *The Politics of Rich and Poor.* New York: Harper Collins.

_____. 2002. *Wealth and Democracy.* New York: Broadway Books.

_____. 2004. *An American Dynasty: Aristocracy, Fortune, and the Politics of Deceit in the House of Bush.* New York: Viking.

Picus, Lawrence and James L. Wattenberger. 1996. *Where Does the Money Go?* Thousand Oaks, CA: Corwin Press.

Piven, Frances Fox. 2004. *The War at Home: The Domestic Costs of Bush's Militarism.* New York: The New Press.

Polyp. 2002. *Big Bad World: Cartoon Molotovs in the Face of Corporate Rule.* Oxford. UK: New Internationalist Publications.

Porter, Gareth & Janet Welsh Brown. 1996. *Global Environmental Politics.* Boulder, CO: Westview Press.

Press, Bill. 2004. *Bush Must Go.* New York: Dutton.

Prestowitz, Clyde. 2003. *Rogue Nation: American Unilateralism and the Failure of Good Intentions.* New York: Basic Books.

Quade, Quentin L. 1996. *Financing Education: The Struggle Between Governmental Monopoly and Parental Control.* New Brunswick, NJ: Transaction Publishers.

Quigly, William P. 2003. *Ending Poverty As We Know It.* Philadelphia: Temple University Press.

Rebell, Michael A. & Joseph J. Wardenski. Jan. 2004. *Of Course Money Matters.* New York: The Campaign for Fiscal Equity, Inc.

Reich, Robert D. 1992. *The Work of Nations.* New York: Vintage Books.

Roemer, J.E. 1998. *Equality of Opportunity.* Cambridge, MA: Harvard University Press.

Roodman, David Malin. 1998. *The Natural Wealth of Nations: Harnessing the Market for the Environment.* New York: W.W. Norton & Co.

Rose, Stephen J. 2000. *Social Stratification in the United States.* New York: The New Press.

Rossotti, Charles O. 2005. *Many Unhappy Returns.* Boston: Harvard Business School Press.

Roy, Arundhati. 2004. *An Ordinary Person's Guide to Empire.* Cambridge, MA: South End Press.

Seabrook, Jeremy. 2002. *The Non-Nonsense Guide to Class, Caste and Hierarchies.* Toronto: New Internationalist Publications.

Schor, Juliet B. 1998. *The Overspent American.* New York: Harper Perennial.

Schrag, Peter. 2003. *Final Test: The Battle for Adequacy in America's Schools.* New York: The New Press.

Sklar, Holly. 1995. *Chaos or Community: Seeking Solutions, Not Scapegoats for Bad Economics.* Boston: South End Press.

Slemrod, Joel & John Bakija. 2001. *Taxing Ourselves.* (2nd Edition). Cambridge, MA: The MIT Press.

Stern, Philip. 1972. *The Rape of the Taxpayer.* New York: Random House.

Strange, Susan. 1996. *The Retreat of the State*. Cambridge, UK: Cambridge University Press.

Swanson, Austin D. & Richard A. King. 1991. *School Finance: Its Economics and Politics*. New York: Longman.

Swanson, Gerald J. 2004. *America the Broke*. New York: Currency/Doubleday.

Tabb, William K. 2002. *Unequal Partners: A Primer on Globalization*. New York: The New Press.

_____. 2001. *The Amoral Elephant: Globalization and the Struggle for Social Justice in the Twenty-First Century*. New York: Monthly Review Press.

Talbott, John R. 2004. *Where America Went Wrong*. New York: Prentice-Hall.

Thernstrom, Abigail and Stephen. 2003. *No Excuses: Closing the Racial Gap*. New York: Simon & Schuster.

Unger, Roberto Mangabeira and Cornell West. 1998. *The Future of American Progressivism*. Boston: Beacon Press.

Upchurch, Carl. 1996. *Convicted in the Womb*. New York: Bantam Books.

Vidal, Gore. 2004. *Imperial America: Reflections on the United States of Amnesia*. New York: Nation Books.

Vork, Victor. 2003. *Sustainable Development for the Second World*. Washington, DC: Worldwatch Institute.

Weisman, Steven R. 2002. *The Great Tax Wars*. New York: Simon & Schuster.

Wilson, William Julius. 1987. *The Truly Disadvantaged*. Chicago: University of Chicago Press.

Wolff, Edward N. 2002. *Top Heavy: A Study of the Increasing Inequality of Wealth in America*. New York: The Twentieth Century Fund Press.

Wong, Kenneth K. 1999. *Funding Public Schools: Politics and Policies*. Lawrence, KS: The University Press of Kansas.

Zepenauer, Mark and Arthur Naiman. 1996. *Take the Rich Off Welfare*. Tucson, AZ.: Odonian Press.

_____. 2004. *Take the Rich Off Welfare.* (New, expanded edition.) Cambridge, MA: South End Press.

> *Let America be America again*
> *Let it be the dream it used to be.*
> —Langston Hughes

Articles

Andrews, Edmund L. "Congressional Study Notes Ways to Collect Billions More in Taxes." *New York Times*, January 28, 2005. p. A15.

Addonizio, Michael F. Spring 2003. "From Fiscal Equity to Educational Adequacy: Lessons from Michigan." *Journal of Education Finance*, pp. 457–483.

Baker, Bruce D. "The Emerging Shape of Educational Adequacy: From Theoretical Assumptions to Empirical Evidence." *Journal of Education Finance*, Winter 2005, pp. 259–287.

Beiser, Vince. "The Rise of the Corporate Plutocrats." *Los Angeles Times Magazine*, October 17, 2004. pp. 10 H.

Belfield, Clive R. and Henry M. Levin. Fall 2002. "The Economics of Education on Judgment Day." *Journal of Education Finance*, pp. 183–205.

Boshara, Ray. "The $6,000 Solution." *The Atlantic Monthly*. January/February 2003.

Brosage, Robert L. *Nation*, April 28, 2003, (pp.4–5).

Browning Lynnley. "Study Finds Accelerating Decline in Corporate Taxes." *New York Times*, September 23, 2004, p. C.3.

Buffet, Warren. As quoted in David Cay Johnston's, "Dozens of Americans Join in Fight to Retain the Estate Tax," *New York Times*, Feb. 14, 2001.

Cavanagh, Sean. "Taxing Plan." *Education Week*, March 3, 2004, p.15.

Citizens for Tax Justice. "Most of Post-2002 Bush Tax Cuts Will Go to Top 1%." April 18, 2002.

Fastrup, Jerry C. Fall 2002. "Assessing State Performance in Equalizing Access to Educational Resources: the Case of Rhode Island (1992–1996)." *Journal of Education Finance*. pp.207–234.

Frank, Ellen. "No More Savings! The Case for Social Wealth." *Dollars and Sense*, May/June 2004, pp. 18–20.

Bibliography

Gale, William G. March 2, 1999. "Americans May Gripe but Taxes Are Low." *International Herald Tribune,* p.9.

Halstead, Ted & Maya MacGuineas. "A Tax Plan for Kerry." *Liberal Opinion Week,* June 7, 2004.

Han, You-Kyung and Richard A. Rossmiller, "How Does Money Affect Teachers' Career Choices?" *Journal of Education Finance,* 30. (Summer 2004) 79–100.

Herbert, Bob, "Educations Collateral Damage." *New York Times,* July 21, 2005, p. A27.

Hightower, Jim ed., "How Did We Get Into This Handbasket?" *The Hightower Lowdown.* Feb. 2003.

_____. "The Rich should Pay Social Security Tax Too." *Liberal Opinion Week,* June 7, 2004.

Hoff, David J. "Texas Judge Rules Funds Not Enough." *Education Week.* September 22, 2004, pp1,30.

Huffington, Arianna. *Los Angeles Times,* July 23, 2004.

Infact, "Hall of Shame." (www.infact.org)

Ivins, Molly. "Tax Dodgers Apply Here." *The Progressive.* Jan. 2003, p.46.

Jackson, Derrick Z. "U.S. Education Suffers in Waste of Iraq War." *Liberal Opinion Week.* May 17, 2004, p.26.

Jefferson, Anne L. "Student Performance: Is More Money the Answer?" *Journal of Education Finance.* Fall 2002, pp. 111–124.

Johnston, David Cay. "A Taxation Policy to Make John Stuart Mill Weep." *The New York Times.* April 18, 2004, p.14.

_____. "A Tax Net that Catches Only Minnows." *The New York Times.* March 6, 2005.

_____. "Richest Are Leaving Even the Rich Behind." *The New York Times.* June 5, 2005, p.1.

Komisar, Lucy. "Offshore Banking: The Secret Threat to America." *Dissent.* Spring, 2003. pp. 45–51.

Krugman, Paul. "Heart of Cheapness," *International Herald Tribune*, June 1–2, 2002, p.4.

Leonhardt, David. *New York Times*, 4-14-04.

Levin, Maurice & Willford Isbell King. 1925. "Income in Various States: Its Sources and Distribution 191, 1920, 1921." New York: National Bureau of Economic Research Inc.

Levine, Betti Jane. "Beware the Ides of April." *Los Angeles Times*, April 7, 2004.

Lindseth, Alfred A. "Adequacy Lawsuits: "The Wrong Answer for Our Kids," *Education Week*, June 9, 2004, p.52.

McIntyre, Robert S. "Loophole – Consolidation Program." *The American Prospect*. December 2003. p.22.

Merl, Jean. "Community Activists Promote Education on Eastside." *Los Angeles Times*, January 19, 2005, p. B2.

_____. "It's Your Money They're Wasting." *The American Prospect,* November 2004. p.16.

Miller, John. "A Rising Tide Fails to Lift All Boats." *Dollars and Sense.* May/June, 2000, p. 42.

Morgan, Dan. "Tax Measures Promise Big Breaks for Business.' *International Herald Tribune.* July 26, 1999. p.3.

Moyers, Bill. "This is the Fight of Our Lives." Keynote Speech: Inequality Matters Forum, New York University, 2004.

New York Times, "Study Finds Gap in Wages and Housing Costs," December 25, 2004, p. A12.

_____. "Long Live the Estate Tax," April 15, 2005, p. A18.

Odden, Alan. Set. 2001. "The New School Finance," *Phi Delta Kappa*, pp. 85–91.

Olson, Lynn. "Kozol Book Puts a Human Face on Fiscal Inequalities." *Education Week.* Sept. 25, 1991. p.1.

Overholser, Geneva, "CEOs Get Richer," *Washington Post.* August 31, 2001.

Bibliography

Pauken, Heidi, "Hit the Road, George," *The American Prospect.* May 2004, pp. 1–8.

Peevely, Gary, Larry Hedges, and Barbara A. Nye. "The Relationship of Class Size Effects and Teacher Salary." *Journal of Education Finance,* Summer 2006, pp. 101–109.

Pierce, Ned. "Tax Largesse and Sharp Accounting: Predictable Winners – and Losers," *Liberal Opinion Weekly,* April 12, 2004. pp. 41–47.

Postel, Sandra & Christopher Flavin. 1991. "Reshaping the Global Economy" in *State of the World.* 1991. Edited by Lester Brown. Washington, D.C.: Worldwatch Institute.

Prugh, Thomas & Erik Asssadourian. "What is Sustainability, Anyway?" September/October, (Vol. 16. No. 5) *Worldwatch,* 2003.

Renner, Michael. 2004. "Moving Toward a Less Consumptive Society." *In State of the World 2004.* Worldwatch Institute. New York: W.W. Norton & Co.

Ritter, Gary W. and Sherri C. Lauver. "School Finance Reform in New Jersey: A Piecemeal Response to a Systemic Problem." *Journal of Education Finance.* Spring 2003. pp.575–598.

Samuelson, Robert J. "The Changing Face of Poverty." *Newsweek,* October 18, 2004, p 50.

Sanders, Ted, Superintendent of Public Instruction and the State (Ohio) Board of Education. July 1995. Report to the Ohio Legislature. "Proposals for the Elimination of Wealth Based Disparities in Public Education."

Scher, Abby. "Corporate Welfare: Pork for All." *Dollars and Sense,* May/June 2000, p.11.

Sloan, Alan. "Why Your Tax Cut Doesn't Add Up." *Newsweek.* April 12, 2004, pp.41–47.

Sullivan, Martin. "U.S. Multinationals Profit from Tax Havens." *Tax Notes,* September 27, 2004.

Teepen, Tom. "The Rich Did Get Richer," *Liberal Opinion Weekly.* August 30, 2004, p.7.

"United For A Fair Economy" 2002 ENNY Awards.

Urich, Roy. "And The Poor Pay Taxes." *The Nation*, June 2, 2003. p.24.

Vieth, Warren. "Firms Often Avoided Taxes." *Los Angeles Times*, April 7, 2004.

Ward, James G. Spring 2003. "A Case analysis of Selected Illinois Rural School Districts: Implications for Rural School Finance Policy." *Journal of Education Finance*. pp.599–605.

Weiner, Tim. "A Vast Arms Buildup, Yet not Enough for Wars." New York Times, October 1, 2004. p. C.1–2.

Wessel, David. "Undoing Tax Cuts." *The Wall Street Journal*. April 1, 2004. p. A.2.

Winter, Greg. "Financial Gap is Widening for Rich and Poor Schools." *New York Times*, Oct. 6, 2004, p A15.

Wright, Jenna. "Wal-Mart Welfare: How Taxpayers Subsidize the World's Largest Retailer." *Dollars and Sense*, January/February 2005, p. 7.

> *The World is too much with us; late and soon,*
> *Getting and spending, we lay waste our powers . . .*
> —William Wordsworth

Biographical Note

Paul Cummins was born in Chicago, Illinois, moved to Fort Wayne, Indiana, and then to Los Angeles, California. He attended Stanford University (B.A., 1959), Harvard University (M.A.T., 1960), and the University of Southern California (Ph.D., 1967). He has taught English at Harvard School and the Oakwood School in California as well as at U.C.L.A. In 1970, he became the Headmaster of St. Augustine's Elementary School in Santa Monica and the primary Founder and Headmaster of the Crossroads School, Founder of New Visions Foundation and PS Arts. He is currently the Executive Director of the New Visions Foundation.

While at New Visions Foundation, he has been the primary Founder of New Roads School, a co-founder of Camino Nuevo Charter Academy, The Los Angeles Academy for Arts and Enterprise, and New Village Charter School. He is the creator of CEO (Center for Educational Opportunity), which places foster children in independent schools, and the Founder of FHF (Families Helping Families), which redirects low income families into life-changing new directions. In addition, New Visions Foundation has instituted an after-school program at Camp Gonzales (a probationary incarceration school) to redirect and relocate juvenile students.

His publications include a booklet on Richard Wilbur, several articles on education, and numerous poems which have appeared in journals such as *The New Republic, Poetry LA, Whole Notes, Wild Bamboo Press, Bad Haircut Quarterly, Wordwrights, Slant,* and others. His biography on Herbert Zipper, *Dachau Song: The Twentieth-Century Odyssey of Herbert Zipper* (Peter Lang, 1992) has been translated into Chinese and German. *For Mortal Stakes: Solutions for Schools and Society,* was published in 1998 by Peter Lang Publishing and Bramble Books and was translated into Japanese, and *Keeping Watch: Reflections On American Culture, Education and Politics* was published by Firstbooks Library in 2002. A collection of poetry, *A Postcard From Bali* was also published in 2002 by Argonne Press. Also an essay, "The Vital Left" appeared in *Fake-City Syndrome* published by Red Hen

Press, 2002. *Proceed With Passion: Engaging Students in Meaningful Education* was published in April of 2004 by Red Hen Press.

He serves on the board of trustees of the New Roads School, P.S. Arts, American Poetry Review, The Gabriela Axelrod Foundation, The Sam Francis Foundation, EXED, The Center for Innovative Education, Camino Nuevo Charter Academy, New Village Charter School, and the Los Angeles Academy for Arts and Enterprise. He and his wife, Mary Ann, live in Santa Monica, California. They have four daughters: Leisl, Julie, Anna, and Emily.